Anti-inflammatory Diet Cookbook For Beginners

1600 + Nutrient-rich Anti-inflammatory Recipes to Reduce Inflammation, Improve Your Health, Slow Down Ageing and Boost Your Immune System With 4-week Diet Plan.

Oliva Lemus Aranda

CONTENTS

Smoothies 47

Salads 54

Sauces, Condiments, And Dressings 63

Introduction

Welcome, dear reader! I am Oliva Lemus Aranda, the proud author of the "Anti-inflammatory Diet Cookbook For Beginners." This book represents my passion and commitment to sharing the transformative power of food and its potential to heal and nurture our bodies.

In my career as a nutritionist, I have often encountered the profound impact of inflammation on our bodies. This subtle yet persistent state can contribute to a multitude of health issues, ranging from heart disease to arthritis, and even to mood disorders like depression. The medical community has made significant strides in understanding inflammation, but I firmly believe, as do many of my colleagues, that the kitchen remains one of the best places to start this battle.

This cookbook is an endeavor to guide you on a journey of understanding and implementing an anti-inflammatory diet. It's not just about recipes - it's about learning to make choices that can help reduce inflammation and promote overall health. Every recipe is a testament to the fact that food, which fights inflammation, doesn't have to be bland or boring; it can be delicious, vibrant, and satisfying.

From hearty breakfasts, colorful salads, nourishing main dishes, to delightful desserts, "Anti-inflammatory Diet Cookbook For Beginners" offers a wealth of dishes that incorporate a variety of ingredients known for their anti-inflammatory properties. But it doesn't stop there. Each recipe also includes nutritional information and tips on what makes these foods a good choice for fighting inflammation.

However, making dietary changes can be daunting, particularly if you're new to the concept. Hence, this cookbook is designed with beginners in mind. It aims to provide a gentle, approachable introduction to the anti-inflammatory diet, making it easy to understand and incorporate into your life.

This journey towards a healthier, inflammation-free life is one of discovery, taste, and above all, self-care. With this cookbook, I invite you to take this step toward a healthier lifestyle, armed with a spatula in one hand, a shopping list of vibrant produce in the other, and a wealth of knowledge to make informed dietary choices. Here's to a journey filled with delicious food that not only satisfies our taste buds but also promotes our overall health. Let's cook, learn, and enjoy together!

With warmth and wellness,

Oliva Lemus Aranda

What exactly is an anti-inflammatory diet?

The anti-inflammatory diet is not a specific regimen but rather a style of eating. The diet emphasizes consuming whole foods, mostly plants, and minimizes processed foods and meats. Here are the key elements of an anti-inflammatory diet:

- **Whole Grains:** Whole grains like oatmeal, brown rice, quinoa, and whole grain bread and pasta, have more fiber, which has been shown to reduce levels of C-reactive protein, a marker of inflammation in the blood.

- **Lean Protein:** Lean proteins, such as chicken, turkey, fish, and plant-based proteins like beans and lentils. Limit red meat and completely avoid processed meats, as they can increase inflammation.

- **Spices:** Many spices and herbs, including turmeric, ginger, and garlic, have potent anti-inflammatory properties.

- **Avoid Inflammatory** Foods: This includes processed foods, sugary drinks, and refined carbohydrates, which can increase inflammation. Trans fats, found in fried foods and commercially baked goods, are also problematic.

- **Hydrate:** Water is essential for overall health and helps flush toxins out of your body, reducing inflammation.

- **Moderate Alcohol**: **Excessive** alcohol can lead to inflammation, so moderation is key.

Adopting an anti-inflammatory diet is more about lifestyle change than a short-term diet. It's about replacing inflammatory foods with fresh, wholesome alternatives, and it's flexible and adaptable to your personal preferences. As always, before making significant changes to your diet, it's a good idea to talk with your healthcare provider or a nutrition professional.

What are the dangers of inflammation?

Inflammation is a vital part of the body's immune response. It's the body's attempt to heal itself after an injury, defend itself against foreign invaders, like bacteria and viruses, and repair damaged tissue. Without inflammation, wounds would not heal.

However, sometimes inflammation persists, day in and day out, even when you're not threatened by a foreign invader. This is known as chronic inflammation, and it can eventually cause several diseases and conditions, including some cancers, rheumatoid arthritis, atherosclerosis, periodontitis, and even Alzheimer's disease.

Chronic inflammation can be triggered by various factors, including an unhealthy diet, lack of physical activity, stress, and exposure to toxins like secondhand smoke or pollutants.

Here are some of the specific dangers associated with chronic inflammation:

- **Heart disease:** Inflammation contributes to plaque build-up in the arteries, increasing the risk of heart disease and stroke.

- **Joint disease:** Chronic inflammation in the joints can lead to conditions like rheumatoid arthritis and osteoarthritis.

- **Lung issues:** Chronic inflammation in the lungs can lead to asthma or chronic obstructive pulmonary disease (COPD).

- **Autoimmune diseases:** Chronic inflammation can trigger the immune system to attack the body's own tissues, resulting in autoimmune diseases like lupus and Crohn's disease.

- **Mental health issues:** Research suggests that chronic inflammation may be linked to mental health disorders, including depression and anxiety.

- **Cancer:** Chronic inflammation has been linked to the development of certain types of cancer, including colon, lung, and breast cancer.

- **Neurological diseases:** Chronic inflammation is thought to play a role in the development of neurological diseases like Alzheimer's disease and Parkinson's disease.

By leading a healthy lifestyle, including eating a diet rich in anti-inflammatory foods, getting regular exercise, avoiding smoking, and managing stress, you can help reduce chronic inflammation and lower your risk of these associated conditions.

What foods should I eat more of on an anti-inflammatory diet?

An anti-inflammatory diet involves eating certain foods that help reduce levels of inflammation in the body. Here are some foods you may want to include in your diet:

- **Fatty Fish:** Salmon, mackerel, sardines, and other fatty fish are rich in omega-3 fatty acids, which are known to reduce inflammation. Aim to eat fish a couple of times a week, and if you don't like fish, consider taking a fish oil supplement.

- **Whole Grains:** Whole grains have more fiber, which can help reduce levels of C-reactive protein, a marker of inflammation in the blood. They are also usually less processed than many other carbohydrate sources.

- **Dark Leafy Greens:** Studies have suggested that vitamin E may play a key role in protecting the body from pro-inflammatory molecules. Dark leafy greens, like spinach and kale, are rich sources of this vitamin.

- **Nuts:** Nuts, especially almonds, are rich in fiber, protein, and antioxidants, and they have heart-healthy fats. They have been found to help reduce inflammation in people with heart disease.

- **Fruits:** Strawberries, blueberries, cherries, and oranges are loaded with antioxidants, which can help fight inflammation.

- **Peppers:** Both bell peppers and chili peppers are rich in antioxidants with strong anti-inflammatory effects.

Remember, everyone's body responds differently to different types of foods, so it's important to pay attention to your own body and see how it responds to the changes in your diet. Always consult a healthcare professional or a dietitian before making any significant changes to your diet or lifestyle.

How can inflammation be properly prevented?

Inflammation is a natural response by the body's immune system to injury, infection, or irritants. While acute inflammation is beneficial for healing, chronic inflammation can lead to various health issues. Here are some ways to prevent chronic inflammation:

- **Maintain a Healthy Diet:** Consuming a diet rich in anti-inflammatory foods is crucial. These include fruits, vegetables, lean proteins, nuts, fatty fish, and whole grains. Minimize intake of processed foods, red meats, and sugary drinks which can contribute to inflammation.

- **Regular Exercise:** Regular physical activity can lower inflammation and boost your immune system. Try to engage in moderate exercise for at least 150 minutes per week or vigorous exercise for 75 minutes per week.

- **Adequate Sleep:** Lack of sleep can contribute to inflammation. Try to get at least 7-8 hours of sleep per night.

- **Manage Stress:** High stress levels can trigger an inflammatory response. Utilize stress management techniques such as yoga, meditation, deep breathing, massage, or other relaxation exercises.

- **Avoid Smoking:** Smoking is a major cause of inflammation. Quitting can significantly reduce inflammation in the body.

- **Maintain a Healthy Weight:** Being overweight or obese can lead to inflammation. If you're overweight, losing even a small amount of weight can help.

- **Regular Check-ups:** Regular health check-ups can help identify issues that might lead to inflammation. Your healthcare provider can guide you on appropriate preventative measures based on your health status.

These preventative measures are generalized and may not work for everyone. Always consult a healthcare professional for personalized advice based on your individual health needs. It's important to remember that these strategies should be part of a lifestyle, not temporary changes. Consistency is key to preventing chronic inflammation.

Breakfast And Brunch

Omelette With Smoky Shrimp

Servings: 2
Cooking Time: 15 Minutes
Ingredients:

- 6 large eggs
- 1½ teaspoons fine Himalayan salt, divided
- 1 teaspoon black pepper, ground
- 1 teaspoon liquid smoke
- ¼ cup Garlic Confit with oil
- ¾ to 1-pound large shrimp, peeled and deveined
- 2 teaspoons avocado oil, divided
- 1 cup arugula

Directions:

1. In a large mixing bowl, place the eggs, ½ teaspoon of the salt, the pepper, and the liquid smoke. Whisk until frothy, then set aside.
2. Heat a 6-inch skillet over medium heat. Place the confit in the skillet when it's hot, quickly followed by the shrimp. Add the remaining teaspoon of salt and for 2 to 3 minutes sauté until the shrimp are pink and begins to coil. Transfer everything from the skillet to a plate. Don't clean the pan.
3. Quickly add 1 teaspoon of the avocado oil, swirl it, and pour in half of the whisked eggs in the same skillet. Add 6 shrimp and half of the garlic, once the bottom is no longer translucent. For 4 to 5 minutes, cover the skillet with a tight-fitting lid and cook.
4. Remove the lid and pick up the skillet to swirl the contents around for 30 seconds. There will be a thin layer of the egg still fluid on the top, and moving it around like this will spread that layer out over the top of the omelet so it will finish cooking while leaving the omelet slightly moist.
5. Run a spatula along the edge of the omelet and slide it onto a plate. Put the skillet back on the stove and use the remaining ingredients to make the second omelet in the same way by adding the remaining teaspoon of avocado oil.
6. Top each omelet with ½ cup arugula and serve right away.

Nutrition Info:

- Info Per Serving: Calories: 403 ;Fat: 21g ;Protein: 42g;Carbs: 5g .

No-egg Mushroom Frittata

Servings: 6
Cooking Time: 45 Minutes
Ingredients:

- 1 small red onion, diced
- 1 ½ cups chickpea flour
- Sea salt and pepper to taste
- 2 tbsp extra-virgin olive oil
- 2 pints sliced mushrooms
- 1 tsp ground turmeric
- ½ tsp ground cumin
- 2 tbsp chopped parsley

Directions:

1. Place your oven to 350ºF. In a bowl, slowly whisk 1 ½ cups water into the chickpea flour; add salt and set aside. In a large cast-iron skillet over high heat, add the olive oil. When the oil is hot, add the onion. Sauté for 3-5 minutes until the onion is softened and slightly translucent. Add mushrooms and sauté for 5 minutes. Add turmeric, cumin, salt, and pepper, and sauté for 1 minute.
2. Pour the batter over the vegetables and sprinkle with the parsley. Place the skillet in the preheated oven and bake for 20-25 minutes. Serve warm or at room temperature.

Nutrition Info:

- Info Per Serving: Calories: 240;Fat: 8g;Protein: 10g;Carbs: 34g.

Morning Naan Bread With Mango Jam

Servings: 4
Cooking Time: 40 Minutes
Ingredients:

- ¾ cup almond flour
- 1 tsp sea salt
- 1 tsp baking powder
- 1/3 cup olive oil
- 2 cups boiling water
- 2 tbsp almond butter
- 2 mangoes, chopped
- 1 cup pure maple syrup
- 1 lemon, juiced
- A pinch of saffron powder
- 1 tsp cardamom powder

Directions:

1. In a large bowl, mix the almond flour, salt, and baking powder. Mix in the olive oil and boiling water until smooth, thick batter forms. Allow the dough to rise for 5 minutes. Form balls out of the dough, place each on a baking paper and use your hands to flatten the dough.
2. Working in batches, melt the almond butter in a large skillet and fry the dough on both sides until set and golden brown on each side, 4 minutes per bread. Transfer to a plate and set aside for serving.
3. Add mangoes, maple syrup, lemon juice, and 3 tbsp of water in a pot and cook until boiling. Mix in saffron and cardamom powders and cook further over low heat until the mangoes soften. Mash the mangoes with the back of the spoon until relatively smooth, with little chunks of mangoes in a jam. Cool completely. Spoon the jam into sterilized jars and serve with the naan bread.

Nutrition Info:

- Info Per Serving: Calories: 625;Fat: 32g;Protein: 7.6g;Carbs: 84g.

Breakfast Bake Millet With Blueberry

Servings: 8
Cooking Time: 55 Minutes
Ingredients:

- 2 cups millet, soaked in water overnight
- 2 cups blueberries, fresh or frozen
- 1 ¾ cups applesauce, unsweetened
- ⅓ cup melted coconut oil
- 2 teaspoons ginger, freshly grated
- 1 ½ teaspoons cinnamon, ground

Directions:

1. Preheat the oven to 350° F.
2. For 1 to 2 minutes, drain and rinse the millet in a fine-mesh sieve. Transfer it to a large bowl.
3. Gently fold in the blueberries, applesauce, coconut oil, ginger, and cinnamon.
4. Into a 9-by-9-inch casserole dish, pour the mixture into it. Then cover it with aluminum foil.
5. For 40 minutes, place the dish in the preheated oven and bake. Remove the foil and bake for 10 to 15 minutes more, or until the top is lightly crisp.

Nutrition Info:

- Info Per Serving: Calories: 323 ;Fat: 13g ;Protein: 6g ;Carbs: 48g .

Ginger Banana Smoothie

Servings: 2
Cooking Time: 5 Minutes
Ingredients:

- 1 banana, sliced
- 2 cups plain yogurt
- 1 tbsp lemon juice
- 2 tsp honey
- 1 tsp turmeric
- ½ tsp cinnamon
- ¼ tsp ginger

Directions:

1. Place the banana, yogurt, lemon juice, honey, turmeric, cinnamon, and ginger in a blender and pulse until smooth. Serve right away and enjoy!

Nutrition Info:

- Info Per Serving: Calories: 235;Fat: 8g;Protein: 9g;Carbs: 33g.

Tropical Smoothie Bowl

Servings: 4
Cooking Time: 10 Minutes
Ingredients:

- 4 bananas, sliced
- 1 cup papaya, chopped
- 1 cup granola, crushed
- 2 cups fresh raspberries
- ½ cup slivered almonds
- 4 cups coconut milk

Directions:

1. Put bananas, raspberries, and coconut milk in a food processor and pulse until smooth. Transfer to a bowl and stir in granola. Top with almonds. Serve and enjoy!

Nutrition Info:

- Info Per Serving: Calories: 840;Fat: 78g;Protein: 19.3g;Carbs: 86g.

Coconut & Raspberry Crêpes

Servings: 4
Cooking Time: 25 Minutes
Ingredients:

- 2 eggs
- ½ cup coconut milk
- ¼ cup raspberries, mashed
- ½ cup oat flour
- 1 tsp baking soda
- A pinch of sea salt
- 1 tbsp coconut sugar
- 2 tbsp pure date syrup
- ½ tsp cinnamon powder
- 2 tbsp coconut flakes
- 2 tsp olive oil
- Some raspberries for garnish

Directions:

1. In a medium bowl, mix the eggs, coconut milk, and mashed raspberries. Add the oat flour, baking soda, salt, coconut sugar, date syrup, and cinnamon powder. Fold in the coconut flakes until well combined. Working in batches, brush a nonstick skillet with some olive oil and add ¼ cup of the batter. Cook until golden brown, 2 minutes. Flip the crêpe and cook on the other side until set and golden brown, 2 minutes.

2. Transfer to a plate and make the remaining pancakes using the rest of the ingredients in the same proportions. Garnish the crêpes with some raspberries and serve!

Nutrition Info:

- Info Per Serving: Calories: 360;Fat: 13g;Protein: 6.3g;Carbs: 56g.

Fantastic Fruit Cereal

Servings: 2
Cooking Time: 30 Minutes
Ingredients:
- 1 cup pineapple, dried and unsweetened
- ½ cup warm water
- 1 cup cashews
- 2½cup coconut flakes
- ½ teaspoon lemon zest
- 1 tablespoon honey

Directions:
1. Preheat oven to 375°F.
2. For 20 minutes, soak the pineapple slices in warm water until softened.
3. Combine with the rest of the ingredients and mix.
4. Spread onto a lined baking tray. Then bake for 20-30 minutes or until crispy.

Nutrition Info:
- Info Per Serving: Calories: 301 ;Fat: 12g ;Protein: 2g ;Carbs: 50g .

Strawberry & Pecan Breakfast

Servings: 2
Cooking Time: 15 Minutes
Ingredients:
- 1 can coconut milk, refrigerated overnight
- 1 cup granola
- ½ cup pecans, chopped
- 1 cup sliced strawberries

Directions:
1. Drain the coconut milk liquid. Layer the coconut milk solids, granola, and strawberries in small glasses. Top with chopped pecans and serve right away.

Nutrition Info:
- Info Per Serving: Calories: 644;Fat: 79g;Protein: 23g;Carbs: 82g.

Sweet Kiwi Oatmeal Bars

Servings: 6
Cooking Time: 50 Minutes
Ingredients:
- 2 cups rolled oats
- 2 cups whole-wheat flour
- 1 ½ cups pure date sugar
- 1 ½ tsp baking soda
- ½ tsp ground cinnamon
- 1 cup almond butter, melted
- 4 cups kiwi, chopped
- ¼ cup organic cane sugar
- 2 tbsp arrowroot

Directions:
1. Preheat your oven to 380ºF. In a bowl, mix the oats, flour, date sugar, baking soda, salt, and cinnamon. Put in almond butter and whisk to combine. In another bowl, combine the kiwis, cane sugar, and arrowroot until the kiwis are coated. Spread 3 cups of oatmeal mixture on a greased baking dish and top with kiwi mixture and finally put the remaining oatmeal mixture on top. Bake for 40 minutes. Allow cooling and slice into bars. Serve.

Nutrition Info:
- Info Per Serving: Calories: 482;Fat: 4g;Protein: 10.7g;Carbs: 101g.

Gluten-free And Dairy-free Little Fruit Muffins

Servings: 2
Cooking Time: 20 Minutes
Ingredients:

- 1 cup almond meal
- 3 teaspoon stevia
- 2 tablespoon ginger, chopped and crystalized
- 1 tablespoon linseed meal, ground
- ½ cup buckwheat flour
- ¼ cup brown rice flour
- 2 tablespoon corn flour, organic
- 2 teaspoon baking powder, gluten-free
- ½ teaspoon cinnamon, ground
- 1 cup rhubarb, sliced
- 1 peeled and diced apple
- ⅓ cup almond milk
- ¼ cup extra virgin olive oil
- 1 free range egg
- 1 teaspoon vanilla extract

Directions:

1. Preheat the oven to 350°F. Line muffin tins using a baking brush or kitchen towel with coconut or olive oil. Into a bowl, put the almond meal, stevia, ginger, and linseed.
2. Sieve the flours over the mix along with the baking powder and spices and stir. Into the flour mixture, add the rhubarb and apple.
3. Beat the egg, vanilla, milk, and oil in a separate bowl until fully combined. Fold the wet ingredients into the dry ingredients until smooth.
4. Into the muffin tin, pour batter and leave a 1 cm gap at the top so that the muffin can rise. For 20 minutes, bake it until risen and golden. Remove then place on a cooling rack before serving.

Nutrition Info:

- Info Per Serving: Calories: 535 ;Fat: 15g ;Protein: 8g ;Carbs: 97g .

Coconut Porridge With Strawberries

Servings: 2
Cooking Time: 15 Minutes
Ingredients:

- 1 egg
- 2 tsp olive oil
- 1 tbsp coconut flour
- 1 pinch ground chia seeds
- 5 tbsp coconut cream
- Thawed frozen strawberries

Directions:

1. Place a nonstick saucepan over low heat and pour in the olive oil, egg, coconut flour, chia seeds, and coconut cream. Cook the mixture while stirring continuously until your desired consistency is achieved. Turn the heat off and spoon the porridge into serving bowls. Top with 4 to 6 strawberries and serve immediately.

Nutrition Info:

- Info Per Serving: Calories: 210;Fat: 27g;Protein: 9g;Carbs: 20g.

Simple Apple Muffins

Servings: 6
Cooking Time: 40 Minutes
Ingredients:

- 1 egg
- 2 cups whole-wheat flour
- 1 cup pure date sugar
- 2 tsp baking powder
- ¼ tsp sea salt
- 2 tsp cinnamon powder
- 1/3 cup melted coconut oil
- 1/3 cup almond milk
- 2 apples, chopped
- ½ cup almond butter, cubed

Directions:

1. Preheat your oven to 400°F. Grease 6 muffin cups with cooking spray. In a bowl, mix 1 ½ cups of whole-wheat flour, ¾ cup of the date sugar, baking powder, salt, and 1 tsp of cinnamon powder. Whisk in the melted coconut oil, egg, and almond milk and fold in the apples. Fill the muffin cups two-thirds way up with the batter.
2. In a bowl, mix the remaining flour, remaining date sugar, and cold almond butter. Top the muffin batter with the mixture. Bake for 20 minutes. Remove the muffins onto a wire rack, allow cooling, and dust them with the remaining cinnamon powder. Serve and enjoy!

Nutrition Info:

- Info Per Serving: Calories: 463;Fat: 18g;Protein: 8.2g;Carbs: 71g.

Avocado, Kale & Cauliflower Bowl

Servings: 2
Cooking Time: 10 Minutes
Ingredients:

- 5 oz cauliflower florets
- 4 kale leaves, chopped
- ½ avocado, chopped
- 1 tsp lemon juice
- 1 tsp extra-virgin olive oil
- Sea salt to taste

Directions:

1. Steam the kale and cauliflower for approximately 5 minutes or until crisp-tender. Transfer the vegetables to a medium bowl. Toss with the avocado, lemon juice, olive oil, and salt. Serve right away and enjoy!

Nutrition Info:

- Info Per Serving: Calories: 320;Fat: 25g;Protein: 7g;Carbs: 25g.

Maple Crêpes

Servings: 2
Cooking Time: 15 Minutes
Ingredients:

- ½ cup almond milk
- 2 eggs
- 1 tsp vanilla
- 1 tsp pure maple syrup
- 1 cup whole-wheat flour
- 3 tbsp coconut oil

Directions:

1. Combine the eggs, vanilla, almond milk, ½ cup of water, and syrup in a mixing bowl. Add the flour to the mix and whisk to combine to a smooth paste. Take 2 tablespoons of the coconut oil and melt in a pan over medium heat. Add ½ crepe mixture and tilt and swirl the pan to form a round crepe shape. Cook for about 2 minutes until the bottom is light brown and comes away from the pan with the spatula. Flip and cook for 2 minutes. Repeat with the rest of the mixture. Serve and enjoy!

Nutrition Info:

- Info Per Serving: Calories: 615;Fat: 40g;Protein: 13g;Carbs: 54g.

Thyme Pumpkin Stir-fry

Servings: 2
Cooking Time: 25 Minutes
Ingredients:

- 1 cup pumpkin, shredded
- 1 tbsp olive oil
- ½ onion, chopped
- 1 carrot, chopped
- 2 garlic cloves, minced
- ½ tsp dried thyme
- 1 cup chopped kale
- Sea salt and pepper to taste

Directions:
1. Heat the olive oil in a skillet over medium heat. Add and sauté the onion and carrot for 5 minutes, stirring often. Add in garlic and thyme, cook for 30 seconds until the garlic is fragrant. Place in the pumpkin and cook for 10 minutes until tender. Stir in kale, cook for 4 minutes until the kale wilts. Season with salt and pepper. Serve hot.

Nutrition Info:
- Info Per Serving: Calories: 147;Fat: 7g;Protein: 3.1g;Carbs: 10.7g.

Yummy Gingerbread Oatmeal

Servings: 2
Cooking Time: 10 Minutes
Ingredients:

- 2 cups steel-cut oats
- 1 tbsp ground cinnamon
- 1 tsp ground cloves
- ¼ tsp grated fresh ginger
- ¼ tsp ground allspice
- ¼ tsp nutmeg
- ¼ tsp cardamom
- 1 tsp honey

Directions:
1. Place a saucepan over medium heat. Add the oats and 3 cups of water and gently stir for 5-8 minutes or until cooked through. While cooking, add the spices and mix. Spoon the oatmeal into a bowl. Drizzle with honey. Serve.

Nutrition Info:
- Info Per Serving: Calories: 390;Fat: 6g;Protein: 16g;Carbs: 68g.

Spicy Apple Pancakes

Servings: 4
Cooking Time: 30 Minutes
Ingredients:

- 2 cups almond milk
- 1 tsp apple cider vinegar
- 2 ½ cups whole-wheat flour
- 2 tbsp baking powder
- ½ tsp baking soda
- 1 tsp sea salt
- ½ tsp ground cinnamon
- ¼ tsp grated nutmeg
- ¼ tsp ground allspice
- ½ cup sugar-free applesauce
- 1 tbsp coconut oil

Directions:
1. Whisk the almond milk and apple cider vinegar in a bowl and set aside. In another bowl, combine the flour, baking powder, baking soda, salt, cinnamon, nutmeg, and allspice. Transfer the almond mixture to another bowl and beat with the applesauce and 1 cup of water. Pour in the dry ingredients and stir. Melt some coconut oil in a skillet over medium heat. Pour a ladle of the batter and cook for 5 minutes, flipping once until golden. Repeat the process until the batter is exhausted. Serve.

Nutrition Info:
- Info Per Serving: Calories: 596;Fat: 33g;Protein: 11g;Carbs: 67.2g.

Smoky Scrambled Eggs With Salmon

Servings: 4
Cooking Time: 8 Minutes
Ingredients:
- 2 tablespoons extra-virgin olive oil
- 6 ounces smoked salmon, flaked
- 8 eggs, beaten
- ¼ teaspoon black pepper, freshly ground

Directions:
1. Heat the olive oil in a large nonstick skillet over medium-high heat until it shimmers.
2. Add the salmon and for 3 minutes, cook and stir.
3. Whisk the eggs and pepper in a medium bowl. Add them to the skillet and cook for about 5 minutes while stirring gently until done.

Nutrition Info:
- Info Per Serving: Calories: 236 ;Fat: 18g ;Protein: 19g ;Carbs: 1g .

Morning Matcha & Ginger Shake

Servings: 2
Cooking Time: 5 Minutes
Ingredients:
- 1 tbsp hemp seeds
- 1 tbsp grated ginger
- 2 tbsp honey
- 2 tbsp matcha powder
- 2 cups almond milk
- 1 cup ice

Directions:
1. Place the hemp seeds, ginger, honey, matcha, ice, and milk in a blender and pulse until smooth. Serve.

Nutrition Info:
- Info Per Serving: Calories: 350;Fat: 8g;Protein: 10g;Carbs: 57g.

Poultry And Meats

Lamb Shanks Braised Under Pressure

Servings: 4
Cooking Time: 50 Minutes
Ingredients:
- 4-6 lamb shanks
- 3 carrots, sliced
- 2 tomatoes, quartered
- 1 garlic clove, crushed
- 1 tbsp chopped oregano
- ¾ cup whole-wheat flour
- 8 tsp olive oil
- 1 onion, chopped
- ¾ cup red wine
- ¼ cup beef broth

Directions:
1. Place ¼ cup of flour and lamb shanks in a plastic bag. Shake until you coat the shanks well. Discard the excess flour. Heat 4 tsp of the oil in your Instant Pot on "Sauté". Brown the shanks on both sides. Set aside.
2. Heat the remaining olive oil and sauté the onions, garlic, and carrots for a couple of minutes. Stir in tomatoes, wine, broth, and oregano. Return the shanks to the cooker. Seal the lid and cook for 25 minutes on "Manual". Once ready, perform a quick pressure release. Whisk together the remaining flour and 8 tsp of cold water. Stir this mixture into the lamb sauce and cook with the lid off until it thickens. Serve and enjoy!

Nutrition Info:
- Info Per Serving: Calories: 800;Fat: 43g;Protein: 73g;Carbs: 20g.

Lemon & Caper Turkey Scaloppine

Servings: 4
Cooking Time: 25 Minutes
Ingredients:
- 1 tbsp capers
- ¼ cup whole-wheat flour
- Sea salt and pepper to taste
- 4 turkey breast cutlets
- 2 tbsp olive oil
- 3 lemons, juiced
- 1 lemon, zested
- 1 tbsp chopped parsley

Directions:
1. Pound the turkey with a rolling pin to ¼-inch thickness. Combine flour, salt, and pepper in a bowl. Roll each cutlet piece in the flour, shaking off the excess. Warm the olive oil in a skillet over medium heat. Sear the cutlets for 4 minutes on both sides. Transfer to a plate and cover with aluminium foil. Pour the lemon juice and lemon zest in the skillet to scrape up the browned bits that stick to the bottom of the skillet. Stir in capers and rosemary. Cook for 2 minutes until the sauce has thickened slightly. Drizzle the sauce over the cutlets. Serve.

Nutrition Info:
- Info Per Serving: Calories: 190;Fat: 14g;Protein: 2g;Carbs: 9g.

Magnificent Herbaceous Pork Meatballs

Servings: 2
Cooking Time: 20 Minutes
Ingredients:

- 8 ounces lean pork, minced
- 1 garlic clove, crushed
- ¼ cup bread, 100% wholegrain crumbs
- 1 teaspoon thyme, dried
- 1 teaspoon basil, dried
- 2 tablespoons extra virgin olive oil
- 1 cup spaghetti, 100% wholegrain or gluten-free

- Sauce:
- 1 tablespoon extra-virgin olive oil
- 1 red onion, finely chopped
- 1 can tomatoes, chopped
- 1 red pepper, finely chopped
- ½ cup water
- 1 tablespoon fresh basil

Directions:

1. In a bowl, mix the pork mince, 1 tablespoon oil, garlic, breadcrumbs, and herbs. Season with a little black pepper and separate into 8 balls, rolling with the palms of your hands.
2. In a pan over medium heat, heat 1 tablespoon oil and add onions and peppers, sauté for a few minutes until soft.
3. Add the tomatoes and ½ cup water.
4. For 15 minutes, cover and lower heat to simmer.
5. Boil your water and cook spaghetti to recommended guidelines.
6. Heat 1 tablespoon oil and add the meatballs to a separate pan, turning carefully to brown the surface of each. Continue this for 5 to 7 minutes before adding to the sauce and simmering for 5 minutes more.
7. Drain spaghetti, portion up, and pour a generous portion of meatballs and sauce over the top to serve.
8. Sprinkle with a little freshly torn basil.

Nutrition Info:

- Info Per Serving: Calories: 435 ;Fat: 23g ;Protein: 37g ;Carbs: 19g .

Chuck Roasted Spicy Beef With Broccoli Curry

Servings: 4
Cooking Time: 50 Minutes
Ingredients:

- 16 ounces sirloin or fillet steak, 100% grass-fed
- 2 tablespoons coconut oil
- 2 garlic cloves, minced
- 1 tablespoon lemon juice
- 1 cup chicken broth, homemade
- 1 cup carrots, chopped

- 1 onion, chopped
- 1 red chili, finely chopped
- 2 tablespoons ginger, grated
- 1 tablespoon black pepper
- 1 cup of broccoli

Directions:

1. Pre-heat the coconut oil and garlic in a large pan over high heat.
2. Add the diced steak to the pan and brown both sides for around 5 to 6 minutes.
3. Take the beef out once brown and leave to one side.
4. Get a bowl and mix the pepper, ginger, lemon juice, and ¼ of the homemade chicken broth.
5. Add the broth mix and the beef back into the pan as well as the chopped onions and chili.
6. Add the last of the stock over the beef and turn down to a simmer for 40 minutes or until piping hot and beef is cooked through.
7. Add the broccoli and chopped carrots into the pan when there are only 15 to 20 minutes left of the cooking time.
8. Serve right away.

Nutrition Info:

- Info Per Serving: Calories: 320 ;Fat: 14g ;Protein: 40g ;Carbs: 8g .

Awesome Herbaceous Roasted Chuck And Scrummy Vegetable

Servings: 4
Cooking Time: 7 Hours
Ingredients:

- 16 ounces chuck roast, lean
- 1 teaspoon pepper
- 2 onions cut, peeled and quartered
- 8 baby carrots, peeled and quartered
- 1 stalk of celery, sliced
- 1 bay leaf
- 10 cups water
- 1 cauliflower, cut into florets
- 5 cherry tomatoes
- Seasoning:
- 1 tablespoon cayenne pepper
- 2 tablespoons rosemary, dried or fresh

Directions:

1. Use a sharp knife to trim any fat from the chuck roast.
2. Season with herbs and spices.
3. Put the onions, carrots, and celery into the crockpot or slow cooker, then the meat, and finally add the bay leaf and water.
4. Cook on low for 5 to 7 hours or until the meat is tender.
5. You can add the cauliflower and cherry tomatoes for the last 15 minutes or until cooked through.
6. Serve hot.

Nutrition Info:

- Info Per Serving: Calories: 170 ;Fat: 5g ;Protein: 22g ;Carbs: 10g.

Korean Vegetable Salad With Smoky Crispy Kalua Pork

Servings: 6
Cooking Time: 10 Hours And 10 Minutes
Ingredients:

- Kalua Pork:
- 3 pounds bone-in pork shoulder
- 1 tablespoon Himalayan salt, fine
- 2 tablespoons liquid smoke
- 1 sweet onion, quartered
- 1 cup water
- 1 banana peel
- Vegetable Salad:
- 4 cups water
- 4 cups chopped watercress, ong choy, or broccoli florets
- 1 tablespoon garlic, minced
- 1 teaspoon fresh ginger, peeled and minced
- 1 tablespoon coconut aminos
- 1 tablespoon coconut vinegar
- 1 tablespoon sesame oil
- 1 teaspoon Himalayan salt, fine
- 1 teaspoon black pepper, ground

Directions:

1. On a flat surface, pat the pork shoulder dry and stand it up with the layer of fat facing up. Score the fat with a very sharp knife, gently cut the slits into a diagonal pattern.
2. Sprinkle the salt all over the pork shoulder, then rub in the liquid smoke until the pork is well covered.
3. In the slow cooker, place the onion quarters. Add the water and banana peel. Place the pork shoulder fat side up on top of the onions. Cook on low for 9 to 10 hours.
4. Transfer the pork to a large bowl when it's done. Remove the bone and use two forks to shred the meat. Spoon 2 to 3 tablespoons of the liquid from the slow cooker onto the shredded pork.
5. Crisp up the shredded pork. Heat a large cast-iron skillet over medium heat. Add the shredded pork in one even layer when it's hot. Let it cook undisturbed for 5 minutes. Stir well, flatten again, and cook undisturbed for 5 minutes more. Then scrape it up from the bottom of the skillet using a spatula and stir.
6. Blanch the vegetables for the salad while the pork is crisping. Bring the water to a simmer in a large pot over medium heat. Add the watercress, garlic, and ginger, cover, and cook for 3 minutes. Prepare a large bowl of ice water. Remove the vegetables from the steaming water and quickly place in the ice bath for 2 to 3 minutes. Drain and pat dry.
7. Place the coconut aminos, vinegar, sesame oil, salt, and pepper in a small bowl. Add the blanched vegetables and gently toss to combine. Serve the crispy pork with this delicious cold salad.
8. Store the pork in an airtight container in the fridge for up to 5 days. Store the salad in a separate airtight container in the fridge for no more than 2 days.

Nutrition Info:

- Info Per Serving: Calories: 536 ;Fat: 36g ;Protein: 44g;Carbs: 6g .

Veggie & Beef Brisket

Servings: 4
Cooking Time: 60 Minutes
Ingredients:
- 4 beef tenderloin fillets
- 4 sweet potatoes, chopped
- 1 onion, chopped
- 2 bay leaves
- 2 tbsp olive oil
- 2 cups chopped carrots
- 3 tbsp chopped garlic
- 3 tbsp Worcestershire sauce
- 2 celery stalks, chopped
- Black pepper to taste
- 1 tbsp Knorr demi-glace sauce

Directions:
1. Heat 1 tbsp oil in your pressure cooker on "Sauté". Sauté the onion until caramelized. Transfer to a bowl. Season the meat with pepper to taste. Heat the remaining oil and cook the meat until browned on all sides. Add the remaining ingredients and 2 cups of water. Close the lid and cook for 30 minutes on "Manual" on High pressure. When cooking is complete, release the pressure naturally for 10 minutes. Transfer the meat and veggies to a serving platter. Whisk the Knorr Demi-Glace sauce in the pot and simmer for 5 minutes until thickened on "Sauté". Pour the gravy over the meat and enjoy.

Nutrition Info:
- Info Per Serving: Calories: 400;Fat: 20g;Protein: 28g;Carbs: 10g.

Pan-fried Turkey Meatballs

Servings: 4
Cooking Time: 20 Minutes
Ingredients:
- 2 tbsp sesame oil
- ½ tsp ground cumin
- 1 ½ lb ground turkey
- 1 cup shredded cabbage
- ¼ cup chopped cilantro
- 1 tbsp grated fresh ginger
- 1 tsp garlic powder
- 1 tsp onion powder
- Sea salt and pepper to taste

Directions:
1. Mix the turkey, cumin, cabbage, cilantro, ginger, garlic powder, onion powder, salt, and pepper in a bowl. Roll the mixture into about 18-20 balls. Warm the sesame oil in a skillet over medium heat. Once hot, sear the meatballs in the pan until browned on all sides, 10 minutes. Serve.

Nutrition Info:
- Info Per Serving: Calories: 410;Fat: 27g;Protein: 2g;Carbs: 5g.

Home-style Turkey Burgers

Servings: 4
Cooking Time: 20 Minutes
Ingredients:
- ½ cup chopped onion
- 1 garlic clove, minced
- 1 ½ lb ground turkey
- 1 egg, lightly beaten
- 2 tbsp almond flour
- ½ tsp chili powder
- 2 tsp minced ginger root
- 1 tbsp fresh cilantro
- Sea salt and pepper to taste
- 1 tbsp extra-virgin olive oil

Directions:
1. Combine the ground turkey, egg, flour, chili powder, onion, garlic, ginger root, cilantro, salt, and pepper in a mixing bowl and mix well. Form the turkey mixture into four patties. Heat the olive oil in a large skillet over medium heat. Cook the burgers, flipping once until firm to the touch, 3-4 minutes on each side. Serve.

Nutrition Info:
- Info Per Serving: Calories: 325;Fat: 19g;Protein: 33g;Carbs: 2g.

Saucy Tomato Beef Meatballs

Servings: 6
Cooking Time: 8 Hours 15 Minutes
Ingredients:
- 1 ½ lb ground beef
- 1 can crushed tomatoes
- 1 large egg
- 1 small onion, minced
- ¼ cup minced mushrooms
- 1 tsp garlic powder
- Sea salt and pepper to taste
- ½ tsp dried thyme
- ¼ tsp ground ginger
- ¼ tsp red pepper flakes

Directions:
1. Combine the ground beef, egg, onion, mushrooms, garlic powder, salt, pepper, thyme, ginger, and red pepper flakes in a large bowl. Mix well. Form the beef mixture into about 12 meatballs. Pour the tomatoes into your slow cooker. Gently arrange the meatballs on top. Cover the cooker and set to "Low". Cook for 8 hours.

Nutrition Info:
- Info Per Serving: Calories: 130;Fat: 9g;Protein: 10g;Carbs: 2g.

Paleo Turkey Thighs With Mushroom

Servings: 4
Cooking Time: 4 Hours
Ingredients:
- 1 tablespoon extra-virgin olive oil
- 2 turkey thighs
- 2 cups button or cremini mushrooms, sliced
- 1 large onion, sliced
- 1 garlic clove, sliced
- 1 rosemary sprig
- 1 teaspoon salt
- ¼ teaspoon black pepper, freshly ground
- 2 cups chicken broth
- ½ cup dry red wine

Directions:
1. Into a slow cooker, drizzle the olive oil. Add the turkey thighs, mushrooms, onion, garlic, rosemary sprig, salt, and pepper. Pour in the chicken broth and wine. Cover and cook on high for 4 hours.
2. Remove and discard the rosemary sprig. Transfer the thighs to a plate using a slotted spoon and allow them to cool for several minutes for easier handling.
3. Cut the meat from the bones, stir the meat into the mushrooms, and serve.

Nutrition Info:
- Info Per Serving: Calories: 280 ;Fat: 9g ;Protein: 43g ;Carbs: 3g .

Mustardy Beef Steaks

Servings: 4
Cooking Time: 60 Minutes
Ingredients:
- ½ cup olive oil
- 2 tbsp Dijon mustard
- ½ cup balsamic vinegar
- 2 garlic cloves, minced
- 1 tsp rosemary, chopped
- 4 (½-inch thick) beef steaks
- Sea salt and pepper to taste

Directions:
1. Combine the olive oil, mustard, vinegar, garlic, rosemary, salt, and pepper in a bowl. Add in steaks and toss to coat. Let marinate covered for 30 minutes. Remove any excess of the marinade from the steaks and transfer them to a warm skillet over high heat and cook for 4-6 minutes on both sides. Let sit for 5 minutes and serve.

Nutrition Info:
- Info Per Serving: Calories: 480;Fat: 3g;Protein: 48g;Carbs: 4g.

Gingered Beef Stir-fry With Peppers

Servings: 4
Cooking Time: 15 Minutes
Ingredients:

- 2 tbsp olive oil
- 1 lb ground beef
- 2 green garlic stalks, minced
- 6 scallions, chopped
- 2 red bell peppers, chopped
- 2 tbsp grated fresh ginger
- ½ tsp sea salt
- 2 tbsp tarragon, chopped

Directions:

1. Warm the olive oil in a skillet over medium heat and place the ground beef. Cook for 5 minutes until browns. Stir in scallions, green garlic, bell peppers, ginger, and salt and cook for 4 more minutes until the bell peppers are soft. Top with tarragon and serve immediately.

Nutrition Info:

- Info Per Serving: Calories: 600;Fat: 20g;Protein: 2g;Carbs: 10g.

Chicken A La Tuscana

Servings: 4
Cooking Time: 25 Minutes
Ingredients:

- 2 cups cherry tomatoes
- 4 chicken breast halves
- 1 tsp garlic powder
- Sea salt and pepper to taste
- 2 tbsp extra-virgin olive oil
- ½ cup sliced green olives
- 1 eggplant, chopped
- ¼ cup dry white wine

Directions:

1. Pound the chicken breasts with a meat tenderizer until half an inch thick. Rub them with garlic powder, salt, and ground black pepper. Warm the olive oil in a skillet over medium heat. Add the chicken and cook for 14-16 minutes, flipping halfway through the cooking time. Transfer to a plate and cover with aluminum foil. Add the tomatoes, olives, and eggplant to the skillet and sauté for 4 minutes or until the vegetables are soft. Add the white wine to the skillet and simmer for 1 minute. Remove the aluminum foil and top the chicken with the vegetables and their juices, then serve warm.

Nutrition Info:

- Info Per Serving: Calories: 170;Fat: 10g;Protein: 7g;Carbs: 8g.

Tangy Beef Carnitas

Servings: 4
Cooking Time: 30 Minutes
Ingredients:

- 1 tsp cayenne pepper
- 1 tsp paprika
- ¼ cup fresh cilantro leaves
- 6 tbsp olive oil
- 4 garlic cloves, minced
- 1 jalapeño pepper, chopped
- 1 ½ lb beef flank steak
- Sea salt and pepper to taste
- 1 cup guacamole

Directions:

1. Place cilantro, 4 tbsp of olive oil, garlic, cayenne pepper, paprika, and jalapeño in your food processor and pulse until it reaches a paste consistency. Reserve 1 tbsp of the paste. Rub the flank steak with the remaining paste. Warm the remaining olive oil in a skillet over medium heat. Sear the steak for 15 minutes on all sides until browned. Remove the meat to a cutting board and let it cool for 5 minutes. Cut it against the grain into ½-inch-thick slices. Put the beef in a bowl and add the reserved garlic paste; toss to combine. Serve with guacamole.

Nutrition Info:

- Info Per Serving: Calories: 720;Fat: 53g;Protein: 2g;Carbs: 13g.

Hot & Spicy Beef Chili

Servings: 4
Cooking Time: 25 Minutes
Ingredients:

- 2 tbsp olive oil
- 1 tsp dried Mexican oregano
- 1 lb ground beef
- 1 onion, chopped
- 2 cans diced tomatoes
- 2 cans kidney beans,
- 1 tbsp red chili powder
- 1 tsp garlic powder
- ½ tsp sea salt

Directions:

1. Warm the olive oil in a heavy-bottomed pot over medium heat. Then, brown the ground beef for 5 minutes, crumbling with a wide spatula. Mix in tomatoes, Mexican oregano, kidney beans, red chili powder, garlic powder, and salt and bring to a simmer. Let it cook, partially covered, for 10 minutes longer. Serve warm.

Nutrition Info:

- Info Per Serving: Calories: 900;Fat: 21g;Protein: 18g;Carbs: 64g.

Classic Sunday Pot Roast

Servings: 6
Cooking Time: 8 Hours 15 Minutes
Ingredients:

- 1 beef chuck roast
- 1 onion, sliced
- 2 carrots, chopped
- 1 celery stalk, chopped
- 2 garlic cloves, minced
- 2 cups beef broth
- 3 bay leaves
- 2 sweet potatoes, cubed
- Sea salt and pepper to taste
- 2 pot roast seasoning mix

Directions:

1. Rub the beef with pot roast seasoning, salt, and pepper. Layer the onion, carrots, celery, and garlic on your slow cooker. Add the broth and bay leaves. Put the meat on top of the vegetables. Put the sweet potatoes on top of the meat. Cover the cooker and cook for 8 hours on "Low". Remove and discard the bay leaves before serving.

Nutrition Info:

- Info Per Serving: Calories: 580;Fat: 30g;Protein: 64g;Carbs: 21g.

Chicken Satay

Servings: 4
Cooking Time: 25 Minutes + Marinating Time
Ingredients:

- 1 garlic clove, minced
- ½ cup peanut butter
- 2 tbsp coconut aminos
- 1 tbsp grated fresh ginger
- 3 tbsp lime juice
- 1 tsp raw honey
- 2 tsp sriracha sauce
- 1 ½ lb chicken breasts, cut into strips
- 2 tbsp olive oil
- 1 tbsp chopped cilantro

Directions:

1. Combine the peanut butter, ¼ cup of water, coconut aminos, ginger, 1 tbsp of lime juice, garlic, and honey in your food processor and pulse until smooth. Set aside the sauce. In a large bowl, whisk the remaining lime juice, cilantro, and sriracha sauce. Add the chicken strips and toss to coat. Cover the bowl with plastic wrap and refrigerate for 1 hour to marinate.

2. Preheat your oven to broil. Thread each chicken strip onto a wooden skewer and lay them on a rimmed baking sheet. Broil the chicken for about 4 minutes per side until cooked through and golden, turning once. Serve with previously prepared sauce.

Nutrition Info:

- Info Per Serving: Calories: 500;Fat: 28g;Protein: 45g;Carbs: 15g.

Rosemary Pork Loin

Servings: 4
Cooking Time: 60 Minutes
Ingredients:
- 2 tbsp olive oil
- 2 lb boneless pork loin
- 1 tsp dried rosemary
- Sea salt and pepper to taste

Directions:
1. Preheat your oven to 375°F. Pour 1 cup of water into a roasting pan. Rub the pork loin with olive oil and place it in a skillet over medium heat. Cook for 4-6 minutes on all sides until browned. Transfer to the roasting pan, sprinkle with rosemary, salt, and pepper, and bake for 40 minutes. Let sit and serve.

Nutrition Info:
- Info Per Serving: Calories: 492;Fat: 20g;Protein: 76g;Carbs: 0g.

Filling Casserole With Cabbage And Sausage

Servings: 6 To 8
Cooking Time: 3 Hours
Ingredients:
- 4 cups water
- 1 large head savoy or napa cabbage
- 1 recipe Pork Sausage, uncooked
- 2 tablespoons butter, ghee, or avocado oil
- ½ teaspoon Himalayan salt, fine
- Leaves from 2 sprigs fresh thyme

Directions:
1. Bring the water to a simmer in a large oven-safe sauté pan with a tight-fitting lid.
2. Fill a large bowl with ice water while the water heats, then core the cabbage and gently pull apart the leaves without tearing them.
3. Put half of the cabbage leaves in the simmering water, cover, and blanch for 1 minute. Quickly remove the leaves and transfer them to the bowl of ice water by using tongs. Repeat with the remaining leaves.
4. Remove the cabbage leaves from the ice water and pat them dry. Save six to eight of the biggest leaves for the top layer.
5. Preheat the oven to 300°F.
6. Pour the water out of the pan, dry the pan, and lightly grease it. Place a thin layer of cabbage leaves on the bottom.
7. Spread one-third of the sausage over the cabbage leaves in a thin, even layer, making sure to spread it all the way to the sides of the pan. Add another layer of cabbage leaf, dot the leaves with some butter, sprinkle with a pinch of salt, and add another layer of sausage. Repeat again.
8. Top the final sausage layer with the cabbage leaves that you set aside for the top, making the thickest layer of cabbage yet. Dot the leaves with butter and cover the pan with the lid.
9. Place the pan in the oven and bake the casserole for 2½ hours. Uncover and bake for 30 minutes more. Remove from the oven and sprinkle with the thyme leaves. Use a large spoon to serve this soft casserole.
10. Serve with toasted slices of Nut-Free Keto Bread or Everything Flaxseed Meal Crackers.
11. Store in an airtight container in the fridge for up to 5 days. Reheat in a preheated 350°F oven, uncovered, for 10 to 20 minutes.

Nutrition Info:
- Info Per Serving: Calories: 452 ;Fat: 36g ;Protein: 27g;Carbs: 2g .

Fish And Seafood

Golden, Crispy, Buttery Pan-seared Cod

Servings: 4
Cooking Time: 10 Minutes
Ingredients:

- 4 to 6 ounces boneless, skinless cod fillets
- 1 teaspoon Himalayan salt. fine
- 3 tablespoons ghee or bacon fat
- 2 sprigs parsley, fresh
- 1 green onion, sliced
- 1 tablespoon Garlic Confit
- Lime or lemon halves

Directions:

1. Pat the fish fillets dry and rub the salt all over them.
2. Heat a large cast-iron skillet over medium heat until it's very hot by rotating the pan halfway every few minutes. Drip water on it for temperature check, if the droplets dance then it's ready.
3. Melt the ghee in the skillet. Add the fish fillets. Be careful not to crowd the pan by cooking two fillets at a time. Sear the fish for 4 to 6 minutes. If the edges of the fish begin to appear opaque white and you can see that it is golden at the bottom by using a thin spatula to flip the fish.
4. Place the parsley, green onion slices, and garlic confit around the fish. Cook for 3 to 4 minutes until the fish is tender and flakes easily with a fork.
5. Transfer the fish to a serving platter. Spoon the ghee mixture over the fish. Garnish with lime halves, if preferred. Let it rest for 3 to 5 minutes before serving.
6. Cook as many fillets to avoid having leftovers. Store leftovers in an airtight container in the fridge for up to 3 days.

Nutrition Info:

- Info Per Serving: Calories: 223 ;Fat: 11g ;Protein: 28g;Carbs: 3g .

Rich Grandma's Salmon Chowder

Servings: 4
Cooking Time: 25 Minutes
Ingredients:

- 2 cans diced tomatoes, 1 drained and 1 undrained
- 2 tbsp fresh chives, chopped
- ¼ cup olive oil
- 1 red bell pepper, chopped
- 1 lb skinless salmon, cubed
- 4 cups fish stock
- 2 cups diced sweet potatoes
- 1 tsp onion powder
- Sea salt and pepper to taste

Directions:

1. Warm the olive oil in a pot over medium heat and place the red bell pepper and salmon. Cook for 5 minutes until the salmon is opaque and the bell pepper is tender. Mix in tomatoes, fish stock, sweet potatoes, onion powder, salt, and pepper and bring to a simmer. Then low the heat and cook for 10 minutes until the potatoes are soft. Divide the chowder between bowls and scatter over the chopped chives. Serve immediately.

Nutrition Info:

- Info Per Serving: Calories: 580;Fat: 43g;Protein: 17g;Carbs: 56g.

Halibut Al Ajillo

Servings: 2
Cooking Time: 20 Minutes
Ingredients:
- 4 lemon wedges
- 2 halibut fillets
- Black pepper to taste
- 2 garlic cloves, pressed
- 2 tbsp olive oil
- 1 tbsp dill, chopped

Directions:
1. Preheat your oven to 400ºF. Place the fish in a foil-lined baking dish. Sprinkle with black pepper and garlic. Drizzle with oil. Bake for 15 minutes until the fish is firm and well cooked. Top with dill. Serve with lemon wedges.

Nutrition Info:
- Info Per Serving: Calories: 490;Fat: 19g;Protein: 55g;Carbs: 3g.

Asian-inspired Salmon

Servings: 4
Cooking Time: 15 Minutes
Ingredients:
- 3 tbsp miso paste
- 1 tsp coconut aminos
- 4 salmon fillets
- 2 tbsp honey
- 1 tsp rice vinegar

Directions:
1. Preheat your broiler. Line a baking dish with foil. Place the salmon fillets on the baking dish. In a bowl, combine miso paste, honey, coconut aminos, and rice vinegar. Rub each fillet with this mixture and broil for 5 minutes. Turn the fillets and rub with the remaining glaze and broil for 5 more minutes. Serve immediately.

Nutrition Info:
- Info Per Serving: Calories: 265;Fat: 11g;Protein: 30g;Carbs: 15g.

Good Old-fashioned Mackerel Risotto

Servings: 4 To 6
Cooking Time: 35 Minutes
Ingredients:
- 8 cups Basic Chicken Broth, or vegetable broth
- 2 tablespoons coconut oil
- 1 onion, finely diced
- 4 garlic cloves, minced
- 2 cups buckwheat
- Four 4 ounces cans Wild Atlantic, King, or Spanish mackerel, drained
- ½ teaspoon salt

Directions:
1. Warm the broth in a large pot set over medium heat.
2. Heat the coconut oil in a second large pot set over medium heat.
3. Add the onion and garlic. Sauté for about 5 minutes, or until soft.
4. Add the buckwheat to the pot and stir for 2 minutes to toast.
5. Add the warm broth, 1 cup at a time while stirring occasionally. Add another 1 cup of broth when all the liquid is absorbed. Repeat until the buckwheat is cooked and tender for 25 minutes.
6. Gently mash the mackerel in a medium bowl to break it up. Fold the mackerel into the buckwheat.
7. Taste and add the salt.

Nutrition Info:
- Info Per Serving: Calories: 594 ;Fat: 31g ;Protein: 43g ;Carbs: 36g .

Scallops With Capers

Servings: 4
Cooking Time: 35 Minutes
Ingredients:

- 2 garlic cloves, thinly sliced
- 1 ½ lb sea scallops, cleaned
- 2 tbsp olive oil
- 1 tbsp capers
- 10 oz fresh spinach
- Sea salt and pepper to taste

Directions:

1. Warm 1 tbsp of olive oil in a skillet over medium heat. Lightly season the scallops with salt and pepper. Pan-sear the scallops for about 2 minutes per side, or until opaque and just cooked through. Transfer to a plate and cover loosely with aluminum foil to keep them warm.
2. Wipe the skillet with a paper towel and place it back on the heat. Warm the remaining olive oil and sauté the garlic for about 4 minutes or until caramelized. Stir in spinach and cook for about 3-4 minutes or until tender and wilted. Top with capers and scallops. Serve warm.

Nutrition Info:

- Info Per Serving: Calories: 230;Fat: 9g;Protein: 29g;Carbs: 9g.

Lime Salmon Burgers

Servings: 4
Cooking Time: 30 Minutes + Chilling Time
Ingredients:

- 2 tbsp olive oil
- 1 lime, cut into wedges
- 1 tsp garlic powder
- 1 scallion, chopped
- 1 lb cooked salmon fillet, flaked
- 2 eggs
- ¾ cup almond flour
- 1 lime, juiced and zested
- 1 tbsp chopped dill
- A pinch of sea salt

Directions:

1. Combine the salmon, eggs, almond flour, garlic powder, scallion, lime juice, lime zest, dill, and salt in a large bowl and mix until the mixture holds together when pressed. Divide the salmon mixture into 4 equal portions, and press them into patties about ½ inch thick. Refrigerate them for about 30 minutes to firm up.
2. Warm the olive oil in a skillet over medium heat. Add the salmon patties and brown for about 5 minutes per side, turning once. Serve the patties with lime wedges.

Nutrition Info:

- Info Per Serving: Calories: 245;Fat: 17g;Protein: 19g;Carbs: 5g.

Honey-mustard Salmon

Servings: 4
Cooking Time: 23 Minutes
Ingredients:

- 4 salmon fillets
- 1 tbsp honey
- 2 tbsp Dijon mustard
- 2 tsp olive oil
- 2 tsp dill, chopped
- Sea salt and pepper to taste

Directions:

1. Preheat your oven to 400°F. Brush all sides of each fillet with olive oil and season with salt and pepper. Place the fillets skin-side down on a foil-lined pan. Whisk together the honey and mustard. Using a brush, coat the top side of the fillets with the honey mustard mixture. Bake for 10-12 minutes until cooked through. Top with dill. Serve.

Nutrition Info:

- Info Per Serving: Calories: 225;Fat: 5g;Protein: 23g;Carbs: 18g.

Autenthic Salmon Ceviche

Servings: 4
Cooking Time: 30 Minutes
Ingredients:

- 1 lb salmon, cubed
- 1 lime, juiced
- 1 Spanish onion, chopped
- 2 tomatoes, diced
- ¼ cup cilantro, chopped
- 1 jalapeño pepper, diced
- 2 tbsp olive oil
- ½ tsp sea salt

Directions:

1. Mix the salmon and lemon juice and let marinate for 20 minutes. Stir in onion, tomatoes, cilantro, jalapeño, olive oil, and salt. Serve and enjoy!

Nutrition Info:

- Info Per Serving: Calories: 230;Fat: 15g;Protein: 1g;Carbs: 4g.

Pan-seared Salmon Au Pistou

Servings: 3
Cooking Time: 30 Minutes
Ingredients:

- 2 garlic cloves
- 1 cup fresh oregano leaves
- ¼ cup almonds
- 1 lime, juiced and zested
- Zest of 1 lime
- 2 tbsp extra-virgin olive oil
- 1 tsp turmeric
- 4 salmon fillets
- Sea salt and pepper to taste

Directions:

1. Spritz oregano, almonds, garlic, lime juice, lime zest, 1 tbsp of oil, salt, and pepper in your blender until finely chopped. Transfer the pistou to a bowl and set it aside.
2. Preheat your oven to 400ºF. Lightly season the salmon with salt and pepper. Warm the remaining olive oil in a skillet over medium heat and add the salmon. Sear for 4 minutes per side. Place the skillet in the oven and bake the fish for about 10 minutes, or until it is just cooked through. Serve the salmon topped with pistou.

Nutrition Info:

- Info Per Serving: Calories: 460;Fat: 25g;Protein: 48g;Carbs: 8g.

Salmon & Asparagus Parcels

Servings: 4
Cooking Time: 30 Minutes
Ingredients:

- 16 asparagus spears, sliced
- 4 salmon fillets
- 2 lemons, sliced
- 1 cup cherry tomatoes
- Sea salt and pepper to taste
- 2 tsp extra-virgin olive oil
- ½ cup hollandaise sauce

Directions:

1. Preheat your oven to 400ºF. Cut 4 squares of nonstick baking paper. Divide the fish fillets between the sheets. Season with salt and pepper, then drizzle with olive oil. Place three lemon slices on each fillet, overlapping them slightly to cover the fish. Sprinkle one-fourth each of the asparagus and tomatoes evenly around the fish and season again with salt and pepper. Drizzle with a little olive oil and wrap up the paper around the fish and asparagus to create parcels. Place on a baking sheet and bake for 15-20 minutes or until the salmon is cooked through and the asparagus are tender. Drizzle with hollandaise sauce and serve immediately.

Nutrition Info:

- Info Per Serving: Calories: 165;Fat: 5g;Protein: 23g;Carbs: 12g.

Mango Halibut Curry

Servings: 4
Cooking Time: 20 Minutes
Ingredients:

- 1 tbsp olive oil
- 2 tbsp mango chutney
- 2 tsp ground turmeric
- 2 tsp curry powder
- 1 ½ lb halibut, cubed

- 4 cups chicken broth
- 1 can coconut milk
- Sea salt and pepper to taste
- 2 tbsp cilantro, chopped
- 1 red chili pepper, sliced

Directions:

1. Warm the olive oil in a skillet over medium heat and place in the turmeric and curry powder and cook for 2 minutes. Stir in halibut, chicken broth, coconut milk, mango chutney, salt, and pepper. Bring to a simmer, then cook for 6-7 minutes over low heat until the halibut is opaque and cooked through. Spoon into bowls and top with finely chopped cilantro and chili slices. Enjoy!

Nutrition Info:

- Info Per Serving: Calories: 430;Fat: 48g;Protein: 1g;Carbs: 6g.

Sea Scallops In Citrus Dressing

Servings: 4
Cooking Time: 20 Minutes
Ingredients:

- 4 tbsp olive oil
- 1½ lb sea scallops
- Sea salt and pepper to taste
- 1 lemon, zested and juiced
- 1 pink grapefruit, juiced
- 1 tbsp raw honey

Directions:

1. Warm 2 tbsp of the olive oil in a skillet over medium heat. Sprinkle scallops with salt and pepper. Place the scallops in the skillet and cook for 6 minutes on both sides until opaque. Combine the lemon juice and zest, honey, remaining olive oil, grapefruit juice, and salt in a jar. Close with a lid and shake well to combine. Drizzle the dressing over the scallops and serve.

Nutrition Info:

- Info Per Serving: Calories: 290;Fat: 17g;Protein: 0g;Carbs: 6g.

Baked Cod Fillets With Mushroom

Servings: 4
Cooking Time: 30 Minutes
Ingredients:

- 8 oz shiitake mushrooms, sliced
- 1 ½ lb cod fillets
- 1 leek, sliced thin
- Sea salt and pepper to taste
- 1 lemon, zested

- 2 tbsp extra-virgin olive oil
- 1 tbsp coconut aminos
- 1 tsp sweet paprika
- ½ cup vegetable broth

Directions:

1. Preheat your oven to 375ºF. In a baking dish, combine the olive oil, leek, mushrooms, coconut aminos, lemon zest, paprika, and salt. Place the cod fillets over and sprinkle it with salt and pepper. Pour in the vegetable broth. Bake for 15-20 minutes, or until the cod is firm but cooked through. Serve and enjoy!

Nutrition Info:

- Info Per Serving: Calories: 220;Fat: 5g;Protein: 32g;Carbs: 12g.

Seared Trout With Greek Yogurt Sauce

Servings: 4
Cooking Time: 30 Minutes
Ingredients:

- 1 garlic clove, minced
- 2 dill pickles, cubed
- ¼ cup Greek yogurt
- 3 tbsp olive oil
- 4 trout fillets, patted dry
- 1 tbsp olive oil
- Sea salt and pepper to taste

Directions:

1. Whisk yogurt, pickles, garlic, 1 tbsp of olive oil, and salt in a small bowl. Set the sauce aside. Season the trout fillets lightly with salt and pepper.
2. Heat the remaining olive oil in a skillet over medium heat. Add the trout fillets to the hot skillet and panfry for about 10 minutes, flipping the fish halfway through or until the fish is cooked to your liking. Spread the salsa on top of the fish and serve.

Nutrition Info:

- Info Per Serving: Calories: 325;Fat: 15g;Protein: 38g;Carbs: 5g.

Mediterranean Salmon

Servings: 4
Cooking Time: 15 Minutes
Ingredients:

- 4 salmon fillets
- 2 tbsp olive oil
- 1 rosemary sprig
- 1 cup cherry tomatoes
- 15 oz asparagus

Directions:

1. Pour 1 cup of water into the Instant Pot and insert the steamer rack. Place the salmon on the steamer rack skin side down, rub with rosemary, and arrange the asparagus on top. Seal the lid and cook on "Manual" for 4 minutes. Perform a quick pressure release and carefully open the lid. Add in the cherry tomatoes on top and cook for another 2 minutes. Perform a quick pressure release. Serve drizzled with olive oil.

Nutrition Info:

- Info Per Serving: Calories: 475;Fat: 32g;Protein: 43g;Carbs: 6g.

Baked Swordfish With Cilantro And Pineapple

Servings: 4
Cooking Time: 20 Minutes
Ingredients:

- 1 tablespoon coconut oil
- 2 pounds swordfish, or other firm white fish, cut into 2-inch pieces
- 1 cup pineapple chunks, fresh
- ¼ cup fresh cilantro, chopped
- 2 tablespoons fresh parsley, chopped
- 2 garlic cloves, minced
- 1 tablespoon coconut aminos
- 1 teaspoon salt
- ¼ teaspoon black pepper, freshly ground

Directions:

1. Preheat the oven to 400°F.
2. Grease a baking dish with the coconut oil.
3. Add the swordfish, pineapple, cilantro, parsley, garlic, coconut aminos, salt, and pepper to the dish and mix gently the ingredients together.
4. In the preheated oven, place the dish and bake for 15 to 20 minutes, or until the fish feels firm to the touch. Serve warm.

Nutrition Info:

- Info Per Serving: Calories: 408 ;Fat: 16g ;Protein: 60g ;Carbs: 7g.

Flavourful Shrimp And Grits

Servings: 4
Cooking Time: 20 Minutes
Ingredients:

- Grits:
- 3 tablespoons coconut butter
- 2 tablespoons ghee, unsalted butter, or lard
- 3 cloves garlic, minced
- 1 piece lemon peel, 1 inch
- 5 cups riced cauliflower
- 1 cup bone broth
- 1 teaspoon Himalayan salt, fine
- Shrimp:
- 1 teaspoon Himalayan salt, fine
- 1 teaspoon black pepper, ground
- 1 teaspoon cumin, ground
- 1 teaspoon fresh rosemary, minced
- ½ teaspoon ginger powder
- 1-pound fresh shrimp, peeled and deveined
- 5 slices bacon, diced
- Juice of 1 lemon
- 2 tablespoons coconut aminos
- Fresh arugula or parsley

Directions:

1. Make the grits by heating a large skillet over medium heat. Add the coconut butter, ghee, garlic, and lemon peel when it's hot. Let the fats melt and come to a simmer. Cook and stir occasionally for 2 to 3 minutes until the coconut butter becomes brown. It will be light brown and smell like toasted coconut.
2. Add the cauliflower and stir to combine. Cook the cauliflower if frozen while stirring often, until it's thawed. Then add the broth and salt. Bring to a simmer and cook undisturbed until the liquid is reduced by half, about 10 minutes.
3. Prepare the shrimp by heating a second large skillet over high heat. Combine the salt, pepper, cumin, rosemary, and ginger powder while it heats in a large bowl. Add the shrimp and toss to coat the shrimp thoroughly.
4. Place the bacon in the skillet when it's hot and cook while stirring often for 8 minutes or until well browned and almost crispy. Add the shrimp and sauté, then stir it often for 2 to 3 minutes until the shrimp have curled and turned pink. Add the lemon juice and coconut aminos and quickly stir to deglaze the skillet and coat the shrimp in the sauce. It should appear browned and caramelized with sticky chunks and lots of crispy bacon.
5. Remove the skillet from the heat. Give the cauliflower grits a stir. It should be creamy without too much pooling liquid. Spoon the grits into four shallow bowls and fish out the lemon peel. To each bowl, add four or five shrimp by making sure to get some chunks of bacon in there, too. Garnish with arugula or parsley.
6. Store leftovers in an airtight container in the fridge for up to 3 days. Sauté in a hot skillet for 3 to 4 minutes to reheat.

Nutrition Info:

- Info Per Serving: Calories: 363 ;Fat: 21g ;Protein: 26g;Carbs: 13g .

Fancy Cod Stew With Cauliflower

Servings: 4
Cooking Time: 30 Minutes
Ingredients:

- 3 cups water
- 1 large cauliflower head, broken into large florets (about 4 cups)
- 1 cup cashews, soaked in water for at least 4 hours
- 1 teaspoon salt
- 1 pound cod, cut into chunks
- 2 cups kale, thoroughly washed and sliced

Directions:

1. Bring the water to a boil in a large pot set over high heat. Reduce the heat to medium.
2. Add the cauliflower. For 12 minutes, cook until tender.
3. Drain and rinse the cashews and place them in a blender.
4. Add the cooked cauliflower and its cooking water to the blender.
5. Add the salt.
6. Blend until smooth. Add more water if you prefer a thinner consistency.
7. Return the blended cauliflower-cashew mixture to the pot. Place the pot over medium heat.
8. Add the cod. Cook for about 15 minutes, or until cooked through.
9. Add the kale. Let it wilt for 3 minutes.

Nutrition Info:

- Info Per Serving: Calories: 385 ;Fat: 17g ;Protein: 36g ;Carbs: 26g.

Saucy And Natural Flavoured Golden Seared Scallops With Wilted Bacon Spinach

Servings: 2
Cooking Time: 30 Minutes
Ingredients:

- Spinach:
- 4 slices bacon, diced
- 1 small onion, diced
- 1 sprig rosemary, fresh
- ¼ teaspoon nutmeg, ground
- ½ pound baby spinach
- 2 tablespoons bone broth
- 1 tablespoon nutritional yeast
- 2 teaspoons garlic, granulated
- ¼ teaspoon Himalayan salt, fine
- Scallops:
- 1 tablespoon lard
- 8 jumbo scallops
- 1 teaspoon Himalayan salt, fine
- ½ teaspoon turmeric powder
- 2 tablespoons coconut aminos
- 2 tablespoons bone broth

Directions:

1. Cook the spinach by placing the bacon in a large skillet over medium heat. Let it cook undisturbed until it begins to sizzle for 3 minutes. Add the onions, rosemary, and nutmeg. Cook while stirring occasionally for 15 minutes until the bacon is crispy and the onions are translucent. Remove the rosemary sprig. Transfer half of the bacon-and-onion mixture to a dish and set for garnishing.

2. Add the spinach to the skillet a fistful at a time and let each fistful wilt before adding more. Mix in the broth, nutritional yeast, granulated garlic, and salt. Bring to a simmer and cook then stir continuously for 2 minutes.

3. In a large bowl, transfer the spinach mixture cover and set aside but keep it close to the stove to stay warm.

4. Cook the scallops. Wipe the skillet with a paper towel and set it back on the burner over medium heat. Let it heat for 1 to 2 minutes then add the lard. Lay the scallops on a cutting board and pat them dry with a paper towel or clean kitchen towel while the lard heats. Rub the salt and turmeric all over the scallops.

5. Once the lard is hot, add the scallops to the skillet. Be sure not to crowd them. Let them sear undisturbed for 2 minutes then use a very thin spatula to scrape carefully and flip them over, revealing a beautiful golden crust. Sear undisturbed for another 2 minutes, then add the coconut aminos to the skillet. Swirl the pan to get the coconut aminos all over the scallops, then use the spatula to remove the scallops from the skillet and set them on two serving plates.

6. Add the broth to the skillet and bring it to a quick simmer. Use a spatula to deglaze the pan. It will lift up any flavor left behind and any aminos that have caramelized on the bottom. Pour this pan sauce over the scallops.

7. Serve right away with the spinach on the side. Garnish with the reserved bacon and onions then serve.

8. Reheating scallops can make them rubbery. Store leftover spinach and bacon in the fridge for up to 3 days.

Nutrition Info:

- Info Per Serving: Calories: 279 ;Fat: 12g ;Protein: 28g;Carbs: 13g.

Vegetarian Mains

Vegetarian Sloppy Joes

Servings: 4
Cooking Time: 30 Minutes
Ingredients:
- 2 tbsp avocado oil
- 2 garlic cloves, minced
- 1 yellow onion, chopped
- 1 celery stalk, chopped
- 1 carrot, minced
- ½ red bell pepper, chopped
- 1 lb cooked lentils
- 7 tbsp tomato paste
- 2 tbsp apple cider vinegar
- 1 tbsp maple syrup
- 1 tsp chili powder
- 1 tsp Dijon mustard
- ½ tsp dried oregano

Directions:
1. Warm 1 tbsp of avocado oil in a skillet over medium heat and place the garlic, carrot, onion, and celery and cook for 3 minutes until the onion is translucent. Add lentils and remaining avocado oil and cook for 5 more minutes.
2. Put in bell peppers and cook for 2 more minutes. Stir in tomato paste, apple cider vinegar, maple syrup, chili powder, Dijon mustard, and oregano and cook for another 10 minutes. Serve over rice.

Nutrition Info:
- Info Per Serving: Calories: 275;Fat: 8g;Protein: 14g;Carbs: 30g.

Teriyaki Vegetable Stir-fry

Servings: 4
Cooking Time: 25 Minutes
Ingredients:
- 2 tbsp olive oil
- 2 red bell peppers, chopped
- 1 onion, chopped
- 1 carrot, chopped
- 2 tbsp teriyaki sauce

Directions:
1. Warm the olive oil in a skillet over medium heat and place in bell peppers, onion, and carrot and cook for 5-7 minutes until the veggies are soft and golden brown. Mix the teriyaki sauce, pour it over the veggies, and cook for 3-4 minutes until the sauce thickens. Serve immediately.

Nutrition Info:
- Info Per Serving: Calories: 170;Fat: 11g;Protein: 3g;Carbs: 18g.

Acorn Squash Stuffed With Beans & Spinach

Servings: 4
Cooking Time: 60 Minutes
Ingredients:
- 2 lb large acorn squash
- 2 tbsp olive oil
- 3 garlic cloves, minced
- 1 can white beans
- 1 cup chopped spinach
- ½ cup vegetable stock
- Sea salt and pepper to taste
- ½ tsp cumin powder
- ½ tsp chili powder

Directions:
1. Preheat your oven to 350°F. Cut the squash in half and scoop out the seeds. Season with salt and pepper and place face down on a sheet pan. Bake for 45 minutes.
2. Heat olive oil in a pot over medium heat. Sauté garlic until fragrant, 30 seconds and mix in beans and spinach; allow wilting for 2 minutes. Season with salt, black pepper, cumin powder, and chili powder. Cook for 2 minutes and turn the heat off. When the squash is fork-tender, remove from the oven and fill the holes with the bean and spinach mixture. Serve and enjoy!

Nutrition Info:
- Info Per Serving: Calories: 240;Fat: 8g;Protein: 3g;Carbs: 40g.

Matcha-infused Tofu Rice

Servings: 4
Cooking Time: 35 Minutes
Ingredients:
- 2 cups snow peas, cut diagonally
- 4 matcha tea bags
- 1 ½ cups brown rice
- 2 tbsp canola oil
- 8 oz tofu, chopped
- 3 green onions, minced
- 1 tbsp fresh lemon juice
- 1 tsp grated lemon zest
- Sea salt and pepper to taste

Directions:
1. Boil 3 cups of water in a pot. Place in the tea bags and turn the heat off. Let sit for 7 minutes. Discard the bags. Wash the rice and put it into the tea. Cook for 20 minutes over medium heat. Drain and set aside.
2. Heat the oil in a skillet over medium heat. Fry the tofu for 5 minutes until golden. Stir in green onions and snow peas and cook for another 3 minutes. Mix in lemon juice and lemon zest. Place the rice in a serving bowl and mix it in the tofu mixture. Adjust the seasonings. Serve warm.

Nutrition Info:
- Info Per Serving: Calories: 435;Fat: 13g;Protein: 6g;Carbs: 66g.

Oat & Chickpea Patties With Avocado Dip

Servings: 4
Cooking Time: 20 Minutes
Ingredients:
- 4 whole-grain hamburger buns, split
- 1 avocado, pitted and peeled
- 1 tomato, chopped
- 1 small red onion, chopped
- 3 cans chickpeas
- 2 tbsp almond flour
- 2 tbsp quick-cooking oats
- ¼ cup chopped parsley
- 1 tbsp hot sauce
- 1 garlic clove, minced
- Sea salt and pepper to taste

Directions:
1. In a medium bowl, mash avocados and mix in the tomato and onion. Set aside the dip. In another bowl, mash the chickpeas and add the almond flour, oats, parsley, hot sauce, garlic, garlic salt, and black pepper. Mix well. Mold 4 patties out of the mixture and set aside.
2. Heat a grill pan to medium heat and grease with cooking spray. Cook the bean patties on both sides until light brown and cooked through, 10 minutes. Place each patty between each burger bun and top with avocado dip.

Nutrition Info:
- Info Per Serving: Calories: 545;Fat: 15g;Protein: 16g;Carbs: 89g.

Cashew & Chickpea Curry

Servings: 4
Cooking Time: 30 Minutes
Ingredients:
- 1 apple, diced
- 2 yellow onions, diced
- 2 garlic cloves, minced
- 2 tbsp avocado oil
- ½ cup vegetable broth
- 1 red bell pepper, chopped
- ½ cup cashews, chopped
- ½ cup golden raisins
- ½ tsp sea salt
- 1 tbsp curry powder
- 2 cups cooked chickpeas
- ½ cup whole milk yogurt

Directions:
1. Warm the avocado oil in a skillet over medium heat. Place the garlic and onion and cook for 2-3 minutes. Add in bell pepper and cook for 5 minutes. Stir in salt, curry powder, and vegetable broth and bring to a simmer. Put in raisins, apple, and chickpeas and cook for another 5 minutes and add in cashews. Top with yogurt and serve.

Nutrition Info:
- Info Per Serving: Calories: 420;Fat: 19g;Protein: 11g;Carbs: 56g.

Traditional Cilantro Pilaf

Servings: 6
Cooking Time: 30 Minutes
Ingredients:
- 3 tbsp extra-virgin olive oil
- 1 onion, minced
- 1 carrot, chopped
- 2 garlic cloves, minced
- 1 cup wild rice
- 1 ½ tsp ground fennel seeds
- ½ tsp ground cumin
- Sea salt and pepper to taste
- 3 tbsp minced cilantro

Directions:
1. Heat the oil in a pot over medium heat. Add onion, carrot, and garlic and sauté for 5 minutes. Stir in rice, fennel seeds, cumin, and 2 cups of water. Bring to a boil, then lower the heat and simmer for 20 minutes. Remove and fluff with a fork. Top with cilantro and black pepper.

Nutrition Info:
- Info Per Serving: Calories: 170;Fat: 7g;Protein: 5g;Carbs: 24g.

Sneaky Fiery Veggie Burgers

Servings: 2
Cooking Time: 15 Minutes
Ingredients:
- extra firm Tempah, 1 pack
- 1 teaspoon red chili flakes
- ½ red onion, diced
- ½ cup baby spinach
- 1 tablespoon olive oil

Directions:
1. Heat the broiler on medium-high heat.
2. Marinate the Tempah in oil and red chili flakes.
3. Heat a little olive oil in a skillet on medium heat.
4. For 6 to 7 minutes, sauté the onion in the skillet until caramelized.
5. Stir in the pepper and baby spinach for 3 to 4 minutes more.
6. Broil the Tempah for 4 minutes on each side.
7. Lay down the Tempah in the buns and then add the caramelized onion, spinach, and diced peppers.
8. Serve immediately while hot with a side of arugula.

Nutrition Info:
- Info Per Serving: Calories: 82 ;Fat: 7g ;Protein: 1g ;Carbs: 5g .

Hot Lentil Tacos With Guacamole

Servings: 4
Cooking Time: 35 Minutes
Ingredients:

- ½ cup red lentils
- 2 tbsp olive oil
- ½ cup minced onion
- ½ cup roasted cashews
- ¼ cup chickpea flour
- 1 tbsp minced parsley
- 2 tsp hot powder
- Sea salt to taste
- 4 coconut flour tortillas
- Shredded romaine lettuce
- Guacamole

Directions:

1. Place the lentils in a pot and cover them with cold water. Bring to a boil and simmer for 15-20 minutes. Heat the oil in a skillet over medium heat. Add the onion cook for 5 minutes. Set aside. In a blender, mince cashews, add in cooked lentils and onion mixture. Pulse to blend. Transfer to a bowl and stir in flour, parsley, hot powder, and salt. Mix to combine. Mold patties out of the mixture. Heat the remaining oil in a skillet over medium heat. Brown the patties for 10 minutes on both sides. Put one patty in each tortilla, top with lettuce and guacamole.

Nutrition Info:

- Info Per Serving: Calories: 500;Fat: 25g;Protein: 15g;Carbs: 55g.

Tofu Caprese Casserole

Servings: 4
Cooking Time: 25 Minutes
Ingredients:

- 1 cup tofu cubes
- 16 cherry tomatoes, halved
- 2 tbsp basil pesto
- 1 cup paleo mayonnaise
- 2 oz grated Parmesan
- 1 cup arugula
- 4 tbsp olive oil

Directions:

1. Preheat your oven to 350ºF. In a baking dish, mix the cherry tomatoes, tofu, basil pesto, mayonnaise, half of the Parmesan cheese, salt, and black pepper. Level the ingredients with a spatula and sprinkle the remaining Parmesan cheese on top. Bake for 20 minutes or until the top of the casserole is golden brown. Remove and allow cooling for a few minutes. Slice and dish into plates, top with some arugula and drizzle with olive oil.

Nutrition Info:

- Info Per Serving: Calories: 475;Fat: 42g;Protein: 8g;Carbs: 8g.

Zucchini & Pepper Hash With Fried Eggs

Servings: 4
Cooking Time: 25 Minutes
Ingredients:

- 4 tbsp olive oil
- 1 onion, chopped
- 1 red bell pepper, chopped
- 4 zucchinis, cubed
- Sea salt and pepper to taste
- 4 eggs

Directions:

1. Warm 2 tbsp of olive oil in a skillet over medium heat. Place in onion, red bell pepper, zucchini, salt, and pepper and cook for 10-15 minutes until the zucchini are tender and browned. Divide the veggies between 4 plates.
2. Warm the remaining olive oil in a skillet. Break the eggs, sprinkle with salt and cook for 3-4 minutes until the whites set. Flip the eggs and turn the heat off. Let cook for 1 minute. Serve each sweet potato plate with a fried egg.

Nutrition Info:

- Info Per Serving: Calories: 390;Fat: 20g;Protein: 9g;Carbs: 48g.

Pesto Mushroom Pizza

Servings: 4
Cooking Time: 40 Minutes
Ingredients:

- 1 cup sliced mushrooms
- 2 eggs
- ½ cup paleo mayonnaise
- ¾ cup whole-wheat flour
- 1 tsp baking powder
- 2 tbsp olive oil
- 1 tbsp basil pesto
- ½ cup red pizza sauce
- ¾ cup grated Parmesan

Directions:

1. Preheat your oven to 350ºF. Beat the eggs, mayonnaise, whole-wheat flour, baking powder, and salt in a bowl until dough forms. Spread the dough on a pizza pan and bake in the oven for 10 minutes or until the dough sets.
2. In a medium bowl, mix the mushrooms, olive oil, basil pesto, salt, and black pepper. Remove the pizza crust spread the pizza sauce on top. Scatter mushroom mixture on the crust and top with Parmesan cheese. Bake further until the cheese melts and the mushrooms soften, 10-15 minutes. Remove the pizza, slice, and serve.

Nutrition Info:

- Info Per Serving: Calories: 335;Fat: 20g;Protein: 16g;Carbs: 27g.

Full Of Flavour Braised Bok Choy With Shiitake Mushrooms

Servings: 4
Cooking Time: 10 Minutes
Ingredients:

- 1 tablespoon coconut oil
- 8 baby bok choy, halved lengthwise
- ½ cup water
- 1 tablespoon coconut aminos
- 1 cup shiitake mushrooms, stemmed, sliced thin
- Salt
- Freshly ground black pepper
- 1 scallion, sliced thin
- 1 tablespoon sesame seeds, toasted

Directions:

1. Melt the coconut oil in a large pan over high heat. Add the bok choy in a single layer.
2. Add the water, coconut aminos, and mushrooms to the pan. Cover and braise the vegetables for 5 to 10 minutes, or until the bok choy is tender.
3. Remove the pan from the heat. Season the vegetables with salt and pepper.
4. Transfer the bok choy and mushrooms to a serving dish and garnish with scallions and sesame seeds.

Nutrition Info:

- Info Per Serving: Calories: 285 ;Fat: 8g ;Protein: 26g ;Carbs: 43g .

Black Bean Burgers

Servings: 4
Cooking Time: 20 Minutes
Ingredients:
- 4 whole-grain hamburger buns, split
- 3 cans black beans
- 2 tbsp whole-wheat flour
- 2 tbsp quick-cooking oats
- ¼ cup chopped fresh basil
- 2 tbsp pure barbecue sauce
- 1 garlic clove, minced
- Sea salt and pepper to taste

Directions:
1. In a bowl, mash the black beans and mix in the flour, oats, basil, barbecue sauce, garlic salt, and black pepper until well combined. Mold patties out of the mixture.
2. Heat a grill pan to medium heat and lightly grease with cooking spray. Cook the bean patties on both sides until light brown and cooked through, 10 minutes. Place the patties between the burger buns and garnish with your favorite topping. Serve warm.

Nutrition Info:
- Info Per Serving: Calories: 420;Fat: 4g;Protein: 4g;Carbs: 75g.

American-style Tempeh With Garden Peas

Servings: 4
Cooking Time: 50 Minutes
Ingredients:
- 16 oz whole-wheat bow-tie pasta
- 3 tbsp whole-wheat breadcrumbs
- 2 tbsp olive oil, divided
- 2/3 lb tempeh, cubed
- Sea salt and pepper to taste
- 1 yellow onion, chopped
- ½ cup sliced mushrooms
- 2 tbsp whole-wheat flour
- ¼ cup white wine
- ¾ cup vegetable stock
- ¼ cup oats milk
- 2 tsp chopped fresh thyme
- ¼ cup chopped cauliflower
- ½ cup grated Parmesan

Directions:
1. Cook the pasta in slightly salted water for 10 minutes or until al dente. Drain and set aside. Preheat your oven to 375 F. Heat the 1 tbsp of olive oil in a skillet, season the tempeh with salt and pepper, and cook until golden brown all around. Mix in onion, mushrooms, and cook for 5 minutes. Stir in flour and cook for 1 more minute. Mix in wine and add two-thirds of the vegetable stock. Cook for 2 minutes while occasionally stirring. Add milk and continue cooking until the sauce thickens, 4 minutes.
2. Season with thyme, salt, pepper, and half of the Parmesan. Once the cheese melts, turn the heat off and allow cooling. Add the rest of the vegetable stock and cauliflower to a food processor and blend until smooth. Pour the mixture into a bowl, add in the sauce, and mix in pasta until combined. Grease a baking dish with cooking spray and spread in the mixture. Drizzle the remaining olive oil on top, breadcrumbs, some more thyme, and remaining cheese. Bake until the cheese melts and is golden brown on top, 30 minutes. Remove the dish from the oven, allow cooling for 3 minutes, and serve.

Nutrition Info:
- Info Per Serving: Calories: 445;Fat: 17g;Protein: 28g;Carbs: 53g.

Tofu Loaf With Nuts

Servings: 4
Cooking Time: 65 Minutes
Ingredients:

- 1 cup chopped mixed bell peppers
- 2 tbsp olive oil
- 2 white onions, chopped
- 4 garlic cloves, minced
- 1 lb firm tofu, crumbled
- 3 tsp low-sodium soy sauce
- ¾ cup chopped mixed nuts
- ¼ cup flaxseed meal
- 1 tbsp sesame seeds
- Sea salt and pepper to taste
- 1 tbsp Italian seasoning
- ½ tsp pure date syrup
- ½ cup tomato sauce

Directions:

1. Preheat your oven to 350ºF. Grease a loaf pan with olive oil. Heat 1 tbsp of olive oil in a small skillet and sauté the onion and garlic until softened and fragrant, 2 minutes. Pour the onion mixture into a large bowl and mix with the tofu, soy sauce, nuts, flaxseed meal, sesame seeds, bell peppers, salt, black pepper, Italian seasoning, and date syrup until well combined. Spoon the mixture into the loaf pan, press to fit, and spread the tomato sauce on top. Bake the tofu loaf in the oven for 45 minutes to 1 hour or until well compacted. Remove the loaf pan from the oven, invert the tofu loaf onto a chopping board, and cool for 5 minutes. Slice and serve warm.

Nutrition Info:

- Info Per Serving: Calories: 525;Fat: 38g;Protein: 25g;Carbs: 28g.

Ultimate Burger With Hummus

Servings: 4
Cooking Time: 30 Minutes
Ingredients:

- 1 tablespoon extra-virgin olive oil, plus additional for brushing
- Two 15 ounces cans garbanzo beans, drained and rinsed
- ¼ cup tahini
- 1 tablespoon lemon juice, freshly squeezed
- 2 teaspoons lemon zest
- 2 garlic cloves, minced
- 2 tablespoons chickpea flour
- 4 scallions, minced
- 1 teaspoon salt

Directions:

1. Preheat the oven to 375°F.
2. Brush a baking sheet with olive oil.
3. Combine the garbanzo beans, tahini, lemon juice, lemon zest, garlic, and the remaining 1 tablespoon of olive oil in a food processor. Pulse until smooth.
4. Add the chickpea flour, scallions, and salt. Pulse to combine.
5. Form the mixture into four patties and place them on the prepared baking sheet. Place the sheet in the preheated oven and bake for 30 minutes.

Nutrition Info:

- Info Per Serving: Calories: 408 ;Fat: 18g ;Protein: 19g ;Carbs: 43g .

Amazing Toasted Cumin Crunch

Servings: 1
Cooking Time: 5 Minutes
Ingredients:

- 1 tablespoon cumin seeds, ground
- 2 tablespoons extra virgin olive oil
- 1 teaspoon black peppercorns, cracked
- ½ teaspoon cumin seeds, whole
- 1 teaspoon cilantro, finely chopped
- ½ jalapeno, finely chopped
- 2 cups of green cabbage, sliced
- 2 cups of carrots, grated
- ½ cup of cilantro, chopped
- 3 tablespoons lime juice

Directions:
1. Get a large saucepan, and then heat the oil over medium heat.
2. Cook the peppercorns, coriander, and the whole cumin seeds for a minute until browned.
3. Add in the jalapeno and then cook for 45 seconds more until tender.
4. Add in then the carrots and the cabbage, cooking for 5 minutes or until the cabbage starts to soften.
5. Add in the crushed cumin seeds and cook for 30 seconds before taking off the heat and then stirring in the lime juice and the cilantro.
6. Serve warm.

Nutrition Info:
- Info Per Serving: Calories: 307 ;Fat: 15g ;Protein: 7g ;Carbs: 44g .

Favourite Pizza With Quinoa Flatbread

Servings: 4 To 6
Cooking Time: 40 Minutes
Ingredients:

- 1 Quinoa Flatbread
- 1 cup pearl onions, halved
- 2 tablespoons extra-virgin olive oil
- 2 cups arugula
- 1 can artichoke hearts in water, 14 ounces

Directions:
1. Prepare the flatbread according to the recipe's instructions. Remove it from the oven when the flatbread is done and increase the heat to 375°F.
2. Toss together the pearl onions and olive oil in a small baking dish.
3. Place the dish in the preheated oven and roast for 10 minutes.
4. Scatter the onions over the crust.
5. Top with the arugula and artichoke hearts.
6. Place the pizza back in the oven and bake for 12 minutes.
7. Cool the pizza slightly before slicing and serving.

Nutrition Info:
- Info Per Serving: Calories: 181 ;Fat: 13g Protein: 4g ;;Carbs: 13g.

Feels Like Autumn Loaf With Root Vegetable

Servings: 6 To 8
Cooking Time: 55 Minutes To 1 Hour

Ingredients:

- 1 onion, finely chopped
- 2 tablespoons water
- 2 cups carrots, grated
- 1½ cups sweet potatoes, grated
- 1½ cups rolled oats, gluten-free
- ¾ cup butternut squash, purée
- 1 teaspoon salt

Directions:

1. Preheat the oven to 350°F.
2. Line a loaf pan with parchment paper.
3. Sauté the onion in the water in a large pot set over medium heat for 5 minutes, or until soft.
4. Add the carrots and sweet potatoes. Cook for 2 minutes. Remove the pot from the heat.
5. Stir in the oats, butternut squash purée, and salt. Mix well.
6. Transfer the mixture to the prepared loaf pan, pressing down evenly.
7. Place the pan in the preheated oven and bake for 50 to 55 minutes, uncovered, or until the loaf is firm and golden.
8. Cool for 10 minutes before slicing.

Nutrition Info:

- Info Per Serving: Calories: 169 ;Fat: 2g ;Protein: 5g ;Carbs: 34g .

Smoothies

Salad-like Green Smoothie

Servings: 1
Cooking Time: 0 Minutes
Ingredients:

- ¾ to 1 cup water
- 1 cup spinach leaves, lightly packed
- 2 kale leaves, thoroughly washed
- 2 romaine lettuce leaves
- ½ avocado
- 1 pear, stemmed, cored, and chopped

Directions:
1. Combine the water, spinach, kale, romaine lettuce, avocado, and pear in a blender.
2. Blend until smooth and serve.

Nutrition Info:

- Info Per Serving: Calories: 180 ;Fat: 10g ;Protein: 4g ;Carbs: 23g .

Lovable Smoothie With Coconut And Ginger

Servings: 1
Cooking Time: 0 Minutes
Ingredients:

- ½ cup coconut milk
- ½ cup coconut water
- ¼ avocado
- ¼ cup coconut shreds or flakes, unsweetened
- 1 teaspoon raw honey or maple syrup
- 1 thin slice ginger, fresh
- Pinch ground cardamom
- Ice

Directions:
1. Combine in a blender the coconut milk, coconut water, avocado, coconut, honey, ginger, cardamom, and ice. Blend until smooth.

Nutrition Info:

- Info Per Serving: Calories: 238 ;Fat: 18g ;Protein: 5g ;Carbs: 16g .

Fresh Berry Smoothie With Ginger

Servings: 2
Cooking Time: 0 Minutes
Ingredients:

- 2 cups blackberries, fresh
- 2 cups almond milk, unsweetened
- 1 to 2 packets stevia, or to taste
- One 1 inch piece fresh ginger, peeled and roughly chopped
- 2 cups ice, crushed

Directions:
1. Combine the blackberries, almond milk, stevia, ginger, and ice in a blender. Blend until smooth.

Nutrition Info:

- Info Per Serving: Calories: 95 ;Fat: 3g ;Protein: 3g ;Carbs: 16g.

Smooth Butternut Squash Smoothie

Servings: 2

Cooking Time: 0 Minutes

Ingredients:

- 2 cups butternut squash purée, frozen in ice cube trays
- 1 cup coconut milk, plus additional as needed
- ¼ cup tahini
- ¼ cup maple syrup
- 1 teaspoon cinnamon

Directions:

1. Release the butternut squash cubes from the ice cube trays and put them in a blender.
2. Add the coconut milk, tahini, maple syrup, and cinnamon.
3. Blend until smooth. Thin with water or more coconut milk if the consistency is too thick to achieve the desired consistency.
4. Pour into two glasses and serve.

Nutrition Info:

- Info Per Serving: Calories: 660 ;Fat: 48g ;Protein: 10g ;Carbs: 59g .

Vegetarian Mango Smoothie With Green Tea And Turmeric

Servings: 2

Cooking Time: 0 Minutes

Ingredients:

- 2 cups mango, cubed
- 2 teaspoons turmeric powder
- 2 tablespoons matcha powder
- 2 cups almond milk
- 2 tablespoons honey
- 1 cup ice, crushed

Directions:

1. Combine in a blender the mango, turmeric, matcha, almond milk, honey, and ice. Blend until smooth.

Nutrition Info:

- Info Per Serving: Calories: 285 ;Fat: 3g ;Protein: 4g ;Carbs: 68g .

Crunchy And Creamy Pistachio Smoothie

Servings: 2

Cooking Time: 0 Minutes

Ingredients:

- 1 cup almond milk, unsweetened
- 1 cup kale, shredded
- 2 frozen bananas
- ½ cup pistachios, shelled
- 2 tablespoons pure maple syrup
- 1 teaspoon pure vanilla extract

Directions:

1. Combine the milk, kale, bananas, pistachios, maple syrup, and vanilla in a blender. Blend until smooth and thick.

Nutrition Info:

- Info Per Serving: Calories: 275 ;Fat: 4g ;Protein: 6g;Carbs: 48g .

Wild Blueberry Smoothie With Chocolate And Turmeric

Servings: 2
Cooking Time: 0 Minutes
Ingredients:

- 2 cups almond milk, unsweetened
- 1 cup wild blueberries, frozen
- 2 tablespoons cocoa powder
- 1 to 2 packets stevia, or to taste
- One 1 inch piece fresh turmeric, peeled
- 1 cup ice, crushed

Directions:
1. Combine in a blender the almond milk, blueberries, cocoa powder, stevia, turmeric, and ice. Blend until smooth.

Nutrition Info:

- Info Per Serving: Calories: 97 ;Fat: 5g ;Protein: 3g ;Carbs: 16g .

Handy Veggie Smoothie

Servings: 1
Cooking Time: 0 Minutes
Ingredients:

- 1 carrot, trimmed
- 1 small beet, scrubbed and quartered
- 1 celery stalk
- ½ cup raspberries, fresh
- 1 cup coconut water
- 1 teaspoon balsamic vinegar
- Ice

Directions:
1. In a blender, combine the carrot, beet, celery, raspberries, coconut water, balsamic vinegar, and ice and blend until smooth.

Nutrition Info:

- Info Per Serving: Calories: 140 ;Fat: 1g ;Protein: 3g ;Carbs: 24g.

Fruity One For All Smoothie

Servings: 1
Cooking Time: 0 Minutes
Ingredients:

- 1 cup packed spinach
- ½ cup fresh blueberries
- ½ banana
- 1 cup coconut milk
- ½ teaspoon vanilla extract

Directions:
1. In a blender, combine the spinach, blueberries, banana, coconut milk, and vanilla. Blend until smooth.

Nutrition Info:

- Info Per Serving: Calories: 152 ;Fat: 5g ;Protein: 2g ;Carbs: 27g.

Fresh Minty Punch With Peach

Servings: 4
Cooking Time: 0 Minutes
Ingredients:

- One 10 ounces bag frozen no-added-sugar peach slices, thawed
- 3 tablespoons lemon juice, freshly squeezed
- 3 tablespoons raw honey or maple syrup
- 1 tablespoon lemon zest
- 2 cups coconut water
- 2 cups sparkling water
- 4 fresh mint sprigs, divided
- Ice

Directions:

1. Combine in a food processor the peaches, lemon juice, honey, and lemon zest. Process until smooth.
2. Stir together the peach purée and coconut water in a large pitcher. Chill the mixture in the refrigerator.
3. Fill four large (16 ounces) glasses with ice when ready to serve. Add 1 mint sprig to each glass. Add ¾ cup peach mixture to each glass and top each with sparkling water.

Nutrition Info:

- Info Per Serving: Calories: 81 ;Carbs: 18g ;Fat: 3g;Protein: 32g;Carbs: 5g.

Light Super Green Smoothie

Servings: 1
Cooking Time: 0 Minutes
Ingredients:

- 1 cup packed spinach
- ½ cucumber, peeled
- ½ pear
- ¼ avocado
- 1 teaspoon raw honey or maple syrup
- 1 cup almond milk, unsweetened
- 2 mint leaves
- Pinch salt
- ½ lemon
- Ice

Directions:

1. Combine in a blender the spinach, cucumber, pear, avocado, honey, almond milk, mint leaves, salt, 1 or 2 squeezes of lemon juice, and the ice. Blend until smooth.

Nutrition Info:

- Info Per Serving: Calories: 248 ;Fat: 14g ;Protein: 5g ;Carbs: 33g .

For Beginners Juice With Granny Smith Apples

Servings: 4 ¼
Cooking Time: 0 Minutes
Ingredients:

- 2 celery stalks
- 2 Granny Smith apples
- 2 cucumbers
- 2 hearts romaine lettuce
- 1 bunch lacinato kale, stems removed
- ½ bunch parsley
- One 1 inch piece fresh ginger
- 1 lemon or lime

Directions:

1. Wash all the fruits and vegetables and pat dry. Juice the celery, apples, cucumbers, lettuce, kale, parsley, and ginger according to your juicer's instructions. Squeeze in the lemon juice and stir. Serve immediately.

Nutrition Info:

- Info Per Serving: Calories: 204 ;Fat: 12g;Protein: 1g ;Carbs: 15g .

Mediterranean Green On Green Smoothie

Servings: 1
Cooking Time: 0 Minutes
Ingredients:

- 1 cup packed baby spinach
- ½ green apple
- 1 tablespoon maple syrup
- ¼ teaspoon cinnamon, ground
- 1 cup almond milk, unsweetened
- ½ cup ice

Directions:

1. Combine all the ingredients in a blender and blend until smooth. Serve.

Nutrition Info:

- Info Per Serving: Calories: 130 ;Fat: 4g ;Protein: 2g ;Carbs: 23g .

Stomach Soothing Smoothie With Green Apple

Servings: 1
Cooking Time: 0 Minutes
Ingredients:

- ½ cup coconut water
- 1 green apple, cored, seeded, and quartered
- 1 cup spinach
- ¼ lemon, seeded
- ½ cucumber, peeled and seeded
- 2 teaspoons raw honey, or maple syrup
- Ice

Directions:

1. Combine the coconut water, apple, spinach, lemon, cucumber, honey, and ice in a blender then blend until smooth.

Nutrition Info:

- Info Per Serving: Calories: 176 ;Fat: 1g ;Protein: 2g ;Carbs: 41g .

Delectable Multivitamin Smoothie

Servings: 1
Cooking Time: 0 Minutes
Ingredients:

- 1 cup red or white grapes
- 1 cup peaches, sliced frozen or fresh
- 1 cup cabbage, chopped
- 1 carrot, peeled and sliced
- ½ cup ice cubes
- ½ cup water
- 1 sprig of fresh mint

Directions:

1. Toss all of the ingredients in a blender or juicer until smooth.
2. Serve immediately in a tall glass with fresh mint to garnish.

Nutrition Info:

- Info Per Serving: Calories: 472 ;Fat: 14g ;Protein: 5g ;Carbs: 86g .

Mixed Berry Smoothie With Acai

Servings: 3 ½
Cooking Time: 0 Minutes
Ingredients:

- One 3 ½ ounces pack frozen acai purée
- 1 cup frozen mango chunks, 1204
- 1 cup frozen berries, 120g
- 2 cups Cinnamon Cashew Milk or Almond Milk, 480ml
- 1 to 2 teaspoons maple syrup or honey

Directions:

1. Defrost the acai pack to soften under hot water. Place the acai, mango, and berries in a blender, along with the nut milk. Start on a low setting, purée the mixture until it begins to break up, stopping and scraping down the sides if needed. Slowly turn the blender speed to high and purée until there are no lumps for 1 to 2 minutes. Taste and blend in the maple syrup, if preferred. Serve immediately.

Nutrition Info:

- Info Per Serving: Calories: 273 ; Fat: 7g ;Protein: 8g ;Carbs: 47g .

Minty Juice With Pineapple And Cucumber

Servings: 3 ½
Cooking Time: 0 Minutes
Ingredients:

- 1 large, ripe pineapple, skin removed and core intact
- ¼ cup mint leaves
- 1 cucumber

Directions:

1. Cut the pineapple in long strips that will fit through the juicer feed tube. Process the pineapple, adding the mint leaves in between pieces, on the proper setting of the juicer. Juice the cucumber, then stir. Serve immediately.

Nutrition Info:

- Info Per Serving: Calories: 9 ;Fat: 5g;Protein: 1g ;Carbs: 2g .

Cheery Cherry Smoothie

Servings: 1
Cooking Time: 0 Minutes
Ingredients:

- 1 cup frozen pitted cherries, no-added-sugar
- ¼ cup fresh, or frozen, raspberries
- ¾ cup coconut water
- 1 tablespoon raw honey or maple syrup
- 1 teaspoon chia seeds
- 1 teaspoon hemp seeds
- Drop vanilla extract
- Ice

Directions:

1. Combine in a blender the cherries, raspberries, coconut water, honey, chia seeds, hemp seeds, vanilla, and ice. Blend until smooth.

Nutrition Info:

- Info Per Serving: Calories: 266 ;Fat: 2g ;Protein: 3g ;Carbs: 52g.

Delightful Smoothie With Apple And Honey

Servings: 2

Cooking Time: 0 Minutes

Ingredients:

- 1 cup canned lite coconut milk
- 1 apple, cored and cut into chunks
- 1 banana
- ¼ cup almond butter
- 1 tablespoon raw honey
- ½ teaspoon cinnamon, ground
- 4 ice cubes

Directions:

1. Combine the coconut milk, apple, banana, almond butter, honey, and cinnamon in a blender. Blend until smooth.
2. Add the ice and blend until thick.

Nutrition Info:

- Info Per Serving: Calories: 434 ;Fat: 30g ;Protein: 4g;Carbs: 46g .

Delicious Proteinaceous Smoothie

Servings: 1

Cooking Time: 0 Minutes

Ingredients:

- 1 cup packed kale leaves, thoroughly washed
- ¼ avocado
- 1 cup fresh grapes
- ¼ cup cashews
- 1 tablespoon hemp seed
- 1 or 2 mint leaves
- 1 cup coconut milk
- Ice

Directions:

1. Combine the kale, avocado, grapes, cashews, hemp seed, mint leaves, coconut milk, and ice in a blender. Blend until smooth.

Nutrition Info:

- Info Per Serving: Calories: 500 ;Fat: 32g ;Protein: 13g ;Carbs: 47g.

Salads

Tangy Nutty Brussel Sprout Salad

Servings: 4
Cooking Time: 20 Minutes
Ingredients:
- 1 lb Brussels sprouts, grated
- 1 lemon, juiced and zested
- 4 tbsp olive oil
- 1 tsp chili paste
- 2 oz pecans
- 1 oz pumpkin seeds
- 1 oz sunflower seeds
- ½ tsp cumin powder
- Sea salt to taste

Directions:
1. Put Brussels sprouts in a salad bowl. In a small bowl, mix lemon juice, zest, half of the olive oil, salt, and pepper, and drizzle the dressing over the Brussels sprouts. Toss and allow the vegetable to marinate for 10 minutes. Warm the remaining olive oil in a pan. Stir in chili paste and toss the pecans, pumpkin seeds, sunflower seeds, cumin powder, and salt in the chili oil. Sauté on low heat for 3-4 minutes just to heat the nuts. Allow cooling. Pour the nuts and seeds mix in the salad bowl, toss, and serve.

Nutrition Info:
- Info Per Serving: Calories: 345;Fat: 29g;Protein: 21g;Carbs: 19g.

Traditional Lebanese Salad

Servings: 4
Cooking Time: 25 Minutes
Ingredients:
- 1 cup cooked bulgur
- 1 cup boiling water
- Zest and juice of 1 lemon
- 1 garlic clove, pressed
- Sea salt to taste
- 1 tbsp olive oil
- ½ cucumber, sliced
- 1 tomato, sliced
- 1 cup fresh parsley, chopped
- ¼ cup fresh mint, chopped
- 2 scallions, chopped
- 4 tbsp sunflower seeds

Directions:
1. Mix lemon juice, lemon zest, garlic, salt, and olive oil in a bowl. Stir in cucumber, tomato, parsley, mint, and scallions. Toss to coat. Fluff the bulgur and stir it into the cucumber mix. Top with sunflower seeds and serve.

Nutrition Info:
- Info Per Serving: Calories: 140;Fat: 8g;Protein: 7g;Carbs: 14g.

Maple Walnut & Pear Salad

Servings: 4
Cooking Time: 10 Minutes
Ingredients:

- 4 cored pears, chopped
- ¼ cup walnuts, chopped
- 2 tbsp maple syrup
- 2 tbsp balsamic vinegar
- 2 tbsp extra-virgin olive oil

Directions:

1. Mix the pears and walnuts in a bowl. In another bowl, combine the maple syrup, balsamic vinegar, and olive oil, pour it over pears, and toss to coat. Serve immediately.

Nutrition Info:

- Info Per Serving: Calories: 280;Fat: 14g;Protein: 4g;Carbs: 43g.

Low In Calories Salad With Artichoke And Almond

Servings: 4
Cooking Time: 0 Minutes
Ingredients:

- 2 cups cooked quinoa
- Two 15 ounces cans water-packed artichoke hearts, drained
- 1 cup kale, chopped
- ½ cup red onion, chopped
- ½ cup almonds, chopped
- 3 tablespoons fresh parsley, finely chopped
- Juice of 1 lemon or 3 tablespoons
- 2 tablespoons olive oil
- 1 tablespoon balsamic vinegar
- 1 teaspoon bottled minced garlic
- Sea salt

Directions:

1. Toss together the quinoa, artichoke hearts, kale, red onion, almonds, parsley, lemon juice, olive oil, balsamic vinegar, and garlic in a large bowl until well mixed.
2. Season with sea salt and serve.

Nutrition Info:

- Info Per Serving: Calories: 402 ;Fat: 16g ;Protein: 16g;Carbs: 56g .

Complementary Spinach Salad

Servings: 4
Cooking Time: 0 Minutes
Ingredients:

- ¼ cup extra-virgin olive oil
- ¼ cup Dijon mustard
- 2 tablespoons lemon juice, freshly squeezed
- 1½ tablespoons maple syrup
- ¼ teaspoon sea salt, plus additional as needed
- 6 cups baby spinach leaves

Directions:

1. Combine the olive oil, Dijon mustard, lemon juice, maple syrup, and salt in a small jar. Cover and shake well to mix.
2. Taste, and adjust the seasoning if necessary.
3. Toss together the spinach and dressing in a large serving bowl.

Nutrition Info:

- Info Per Serving: Calories: 150 ;Fat: 14g ;Protein: 2g ;Carbs: 8g .

High-spirited Salmon Salad

Servings: 2
Cooking Time: 0 Minutes
Ingredients:
- 3 cups baby spinach
- ½ cucumber, thinly sliced
- 1 small fennel bulb, trimmed and thinly sliced
- 2 leftover Basic Baked Salmon fillets, flaked
- 1 small ripe avocado, peeled, pitted, and sliced
- ¼ cup extra-virgin olive oil
- 2 tablespoons lemon juice, fresh
- 1 teaspoon salt
- ¼ teaspoon black pepper, freshly ground
- 1 teaspoon fresh dill, chopped

Directions:
1. Arrange the spinach on a serving platter or in a bowl.
2. Top with the cucumber, fennel, salmon, and avocado.
3. Whisk together the olive oil, lemon juice, salt, pepper, and dill in a small bowl or shake in a small jar with a tight-fitting lid.
4. Pour the dressing over the salad, and serve.

Nutrition Info:
- Info Per Serving: Calories: 590 ;Fat: 48g ;Protein: 23g ;Carbs: 20g .

Lemony Spinach Salad

Servings: 4
Cooking Time: 10 Minutes
Ingredients:
- 2 tbsp pine nuts, toasted
- 6 cups baby spinach
- 2 tbsp lemon juice
- ¼ cup Dijon mustard
- 1 ½ tbsp maple syrup
- 2 tbsp extra-virgin olive oil
- Sea salt to taste

Directions:
1. Combine all the ingredients, except for the spinach and pine nuts, in a small bowl. Mix well. Put the spinach in a large serving bowl, drizzle with the lemon dressing, toss to combine well. Top with pine nuts and serve.

Nutrition Info:
- Info Per Serving: Calories: 155;Fat: 15g;Protein: 2g;Carbs: 8g.

Gratifying Healthy Sweet Potato Salad With Mustard And Tarragon

Servings: 2
Cooking Time: 30 Minutes
Ingredients:

- 2 medium-sized sweet potatoes, peeled and cubed
- 2½cup of low-fat Greek yogurt
- 2 tablespoons Dijon mustard
- 1 tablespoon tarragon, dried
- 1 beef tomato, finely chopped
- 2½ yellow pepper, finely chopped
- ½ red onion, finely chopped
- pinch of black pepper

Directions:

1. Boil water in a large pot on high heat.
2. Cook the potatoes in the pot for 20 minutes or until tender.
3. After draining, set aside to cool down.
4. In a serving bowl, combine Dijon mustard, plain yogurt, tarragon, peppers, tomatoes, and red onion.
5. Add the cooled potatoes and mix well then serve.

Nutrition Info:

- Info Per Serving: Calories: 260 ;Fat: 3g ;Protein: 12g ;Carbs: 50g.

Orange & Kale Salad

Servings: 4
Cooking Time: 10 Minutes
Ingredients:

- 2 tbsp Dijon mustard
- 2 tbsp olive oil
- ¼ cup fresh orange juice
- 1 tsp honey
- 2 tbsp minced fresh parsley
- 1 tbsp minced green onions
- 4 cups fresh kale, chopped
- 1 peeled orange, segmented
- ½ red onion, sliced thin
- Sea salt and pepper to taste

Directions:

1. Blend the mustard, oil, orange juice, honey, salt, pepper, parsley, and green onions in your food processor until smooth. Set aside. In a bowl, combine the kale, orange, and onion. Pour over the dressing and toss to coat. Serve.

Nutrition Info:

- Info Per Serving: Calories: 105;Fat: 7g;Protein: 1g;Carbs: 10g.

Refreshingly Spicy Chicken Salad With Cumin And Mango

Servings: 2
Cooking Time: 15 Minutes
Ingredients:

- 2 free range chicken breasts, skinless
- 1 teaspoon oregano, finely chopped
- 1 garlic clove, minced
- 1 teaspoon chili flakes
- 1 teaspoon cumin
- 1 teaspoon turmeric
- 1 tablespoon extra-virgin olive oil
- 1 lime, juiced
- 1 cup mango, cubed
- ½ iceberg/romaine lettuce or similar, sliced

Directions:

1. Mix oil, garlic, herbs, and spices with the lime juice in a bowl.
2. Add the chicken and marinate for at least 30 minutes up to overnight.
3. Preheat the broiler when ready to serve to medium-high heat.
4. Add the chicken to a lightly greased baking tray and broil for 10-12 minutes or until cooked through.
5. In a serving bowl, combine the lettuce with the mango.
6. Serve immediately once the chicken is cooked on top of the mango and lettuce.

Nutrition Info:

- Info Per Serving: Calories: 216 ;Fat: 9g ;Protein: 19g ;Carbs: 19g .

The Best Mediterranean Salad

Servings: 4
Cooking Time: 15 Minutes
Ingredients:

- 2 green onions, sliced
- 2 garlic cloves, minced
- 2 cups packed spinach
- 3 large tomatoes, diced
- 1 bunch radishes, sliced
- 1 peeled cucumber, diced
- 1 tbsp chopped fresh mint
- 1 tbsp chopped parsley
- 1 cup plain almond yogurt
- 1 tbsp apple cider vinegar
- 3 tbsp lemon juice
- 1 tbsp sumac
- 2 tbsp extra-virgin olive oil
- Sea salt and pepper to taste

Directions:

1. Place all the ingredients in a large salad bowl and toss to coat well. Serve immediately.

Nutrition Info:

- Info Per Serving: Calories: 200;Fat: 15g;Protein: 5g;Carbs: 15g.

Carrot & Cabbage Salad With Avocado

Servings: 4
Cooking Time: 15 Minutes
Ingredients:
- 1 carrot, shredded
- 1 cup shredded red cabbage
- 16 cherry tomatoes, halved
- 1 red bell pepper, sliced
- 1 can chickpeas
- ¼ cup capers
- 1 avocado, sliced
- ¼ cup olive oil
- 1 ½ tbsp fresh lemon juice
- Sea salt and pepper to taste

Directions:
1. Mix the oil, lemon juice, salt, and pepper until combined in a bowl. Add carrot, cabbage, tomatoes, bell pepper, chickpeas, capers, and avocado and toss to coat. Serve.

Nutrition Info:
- Info Per Serving: Calories: 325;Fat: 23g;Protein: 7g;Carbs: 28g.

Warm Collard Salad

Servings: 2
Cooking Time: 10 Minutes
Ingredients:
- ¾ cup coconut whipping cream
- 2 tbsp paleo mayonnaise
- A pinch of mustard powder
- 2 tbsp coconut oil
- 1 garlic clove, minced
- Sea salt and pepper to taste
- 2 oz olive oil
- 1 cup collards, rinsed
- 4 oz tofu, cubed

Directions:
1. In a small bowl, whisk the coconut whipping cream, mayonnaise, mustard powder, coconut oil, garlic, salt, and black pepper until well mixed; set aside. Warm the olive oil in a large skillet over medium heat and sauté the collards until wilted and brownish. Season with salt and black pepper to taste. Transfer the collards to a salad bowl and pour the creamy dressing over. Mix the salad well and crumble the tofu over. Serve.

Nutrition Info:
- Info Per Serving: Calories: 570;Fat: 57g;Protein: 13g;Carbs: 8g.

Mushroom & Wild Rice Salad

Servings: 6
Cooking Time: 25 Minutes
Ingredients:

- 2 cups cremini mushrooms, sliced
- 2 garlic cloves, minced
- 1 sweet onion, diced
- 3 cups wild rice, cooked
- 2 tbsp avocado oil
- ½ tsp dried thyme
- ½ cup vegetable broth
- ½ tsp sea salt

Directions:

1. Place the wild rice in a bowl and set aside. Warm the avocado oil in a saucepan over medium heat. Place the garlic and onion and cook for 5 minutes, stirring often. Mix in vegetable broth, thyme, salt, and mushrooms and cook for 10 minutes until the mushrooms are tender and the broth reduces by half. Stir in wild rice. Serve.

Nutrition Info:

- Info Per Serving: Calories: 145;Fat: 1g;Protein: 20g;Carbs: 5g.

Chinese-style Cabbage Salad

Servings: 6
Cooking Time: 15 Minutes
Ingredients:

- 4 cups shredded red cabbage
- 2 cups sliced white cabbage
- 1 cup red radishes, sliced
- ¼ cup fresh orange juice
- 2 tbsp Chinese black vinegar
- 1 tsp low-sodium soy sauce
- 2 tbsp olive oil
- 1 tsp grated fresh ginger
- 1 tbsp black sesame seeds

Directions:

1. Mix the red cabbage, white cabbage, and radishes in a bowl. In another bowl, whisk the orange juice, vinegar, soy sauce, olive oil, and ginger. Pour over the slaw and toss to coat. Marinate covered in the fridge for 2 hours. Serve topped with sesame seeds.

Nutrition Info:

- Info Per Serving: Calories: 80;Fat: 6g;Protein: 2g;Carbs: 7g.

Fantastic Green Salad

Servings: 4
Cooking Time: 10 Minutes
Ingredients:

- 1 head Iceberg lettuce
- 8 asparagus, chopped
- 2 seedless cucumbers, sliced
- 1 zucchini, cut into ribbons
- 1 carrot, cut into ribbons
- 1 avocado, sliced
- ½ cup green dressing
- 2 scallions, thinly sliced

Directions:

1. Share the lettuce into 4 bowls and add in some asparagus, cucumber, zucchini, carrot, and avocado. Sprinkle each bowl with 2 tbsp of dressing. Serve topped with scallions.

Nutrition Info:

- Info Per Serving: Calories: 255;Fat: 21g;Protein: 4g;Carbs: 15g.

Traditional Middle Eastern Chopped Salad

Servings: 4
Cooking Time: 0 Minutes
Ingredients:

- 2 cups packed spinach
- 3 large tomatoes, diced
- 1 bunch radishes, sliced thin
- 1 English cucumber, peeled and diced
- 2 scallions, sliced
- 2 garlic cloves, minced
- 1 tablespoon fresh mint, chopped
- 1 tablespoon fresh parsley, chopped

- 1 cup plain almond yogurt, unsweetened
- ¼ cup extra-virgin olive oil
- 3 tablespoons lemon juice, freshly squeezed
- 1 tablespoon apple cider vinegar
- 1 teaspoon sea salt
- ¼ teaspoon black pepper, freshly ground
- 1 tablespoon sumac

Directions:

1. Combine the spinach, tomatoes, radishes, cucumber, scallions, garlic, mint, parsley, yogurt, olive oil, lemon juice, cider vinegar, salt, pepper, and sumacin a large bowl. Toss to combine.
2. Serve and enjoy.

Nutrition Info:

- Info Per Serving: Calories: 194 ;Fat: 14g ;Protein: 4g ;Carbs: 15g .

Diverse Salad With Shredded Root Vegetable

Servings: 4
Cooking Time: 0 Minutes
Ingredients:

- Dressing:
- ¼ cup olive oil
- 3 tablespoons pure maple syrup
- 2 tablespoons apple cider vinegar
- 1 teaspoon fresh ginger, grated
- Sea salt
- Slaw:
- 1 jicama, or 2 parsnips, peeled and shredded
- 2 carrots, shredded, or 1 cup pre-shredded packaged carrots
- ½ celeriac, peeled and shredded
- ¼ fennel bulb, shredded
- 5 radishes, shredded
- 2 scallions, white and green parts, peeled and thinly sliced
- ½ cup pumpkin seeds, roasted

Directions:

1. Whisk the olive oil, maple syrup, cider vinegar, and ginger in a small bowl until well blended. Season with sea salt and set it aside.
2. Toss together the jicama, carrots, celeriac, fennel, radishes, and scallions in a large bowl.
3. Add the dressing and toss to coat.
4. Top the slaw with the pumpkin seeds and serve.

Nutrition Info:

- Info Per Serving: Calories: 343 ;Fat: 21g ;Protein: 7g;Carbs: 36g .

Minty Salad With Melon

Servings: 4
Cooking Time: 0 Minutes
Ingredients:
- Dressing:
- 3 tablespoons olive oil
- 2 tablespoons red wine vinegar
- Sea salt
- Salad:
- 1 honeydew melon, rind removed, flesh cut into 1-inch cubes
- ½ cantaloupe, rind removed, flesh cut into 1-inch cubes
- 3 stalks celery, sliced, or about 1 to 1½ cups precut packaged celery
- ½ red onion, thinly sliced
- ¼ cup fresh mint, chopped

Directions:
1. Whisk the olive oil and red wine vinegar in a small bowl. Season with sea salt and set it aside.
2. Combine the honeydew, cantaloupe, celery, red onion, and mint in a large bowl.
3. Add the dressing and toss to combine

Nutrition Info:
- Info Per Serving: Calories: 223 ;Fat: 11g ;Protein: 2g;Carbs: 32g .

Soy-free Salad With Chopped Chicken And Apple

Servings: 2
Cooking Time: 0 Minutes
Ingredients:
- 2 cooked boneless, skinless chicken breasts, cut into ½-inch cubes
- ½ cup celery, chopped
- 1 large green apple, cored and coarsely chopped
- 1 romaine lettuce heart, chopped
- 3 scallions, chopped
- ½ cup canned chickpeas
- ½ cup Lemony Mustard Dressing

Directions:
1. In a large bowl, combine the chicken, celery, apple, romaine, scallions, and chickpeas.
2. Add the dressing and toss to mix.
3. Divide the salad among four serving bowls, top with the toasted walnuts (if using), and serve.

Nutrition Info:
- Info Per Serving: Calories: 860 ;Fat: 61g ;Protein: 45g ;Carbs: 39g .

Sauces, Condiments, And Dressings

Commercial And Mild Curry Powder

Servings: ¼
Cooking Time: 0 Minutes
Ingredients:
- 1 tablespoon turmeric, ground
- 1 tablespoon cumin, ground
- 2 teaspoons coriander, ground
- 1 teaspoon cardamom, ground
- 1 teaspoon cinnamon, ground
- 1 teaspoon ginger, ground
- ½ teaspoon fenugreek powder
- ½ teaspoon cloves, ground

Directions:
1. Stir together in a small bowl the turmeric, cumin, coriander, cardamom, cinnamon, ginger, fenugreek, and cloves until fully blended.
2. Store the curry powder in an airtight container for up to 1 month.

Nutrition Info:
- Info Per Serving: Calories: 6 ;Fat: 15g;Protein: 46g;Carbs: 1g.

Colourful Fiesta Guacamole

Servings: 3
Cooking Time: 0 Minutes
Ingredients:
- 3 medium Hass avocados, halved, pitted, and peeled
- 3 small radishes, sliced
- 3 large strawberries, diced
- 3 cloves garlic, minced
- 1 green onion, sliced
- ½ bunch fresh cilantro, minced and 1½ ounces
- Juice of 2 lemons
- 2 teaspoons Himalayan salt, fine
- 1 tablespoon extra-virgin olive oil

Directions:
1. In a large bowl, place all the ingredients. Use a whisk or pestle to mix and mash them together until you have chunky guacamole.
2. Transfer it to an airtight container, drizzle olive oil on it, set a sheet of plastic wrap on the top so that it sticks directly to the guacamole, and put the lid on. Store in the fridge until ready to enjoy, but no more than 4 days.

Nutrition Info:
- Info Per Serving: Calories: 215 ;Fat: 18g ;Protein: 4g;Carbs: 15g .

Traditional And Delightful Gremolata Sauce

Servings: 1
Cooking Time: 0 Minutes
Ingredients:

- ¾ cup finely fresh parsley, chopped
- Juice of 2 lemons or 6 tablespoons
- Zest of 2 lemons
- 2 tablespoons olive oil
- 2 teaspoons minced garlic, bottled
- ¼ teaspoon sea salt

Directions:

1. Stir together in a small bowl the parsley, lemon juice, lemon zest, olive oil, garlic, and sea salt until well blended.
2. Refrigerate in a sealed container for up to 4 days.

Nutrition Info:

- Info Per Serving: Calories: 33 ;Fat: 4g ;Protein: 46g;Carbs: 1g.

Sour Cream With Lemon And Dill

Servings: 3
Cooking Time: 15 Minutes
Ingredients:

- ¾ cup cashews, soaked in water for 4 hours
- ¼ cup water
- Juice of 1 lemon
- Zest of 1 lemon
- 2 tablespoons fresh dill, chopped
- ¼ teaspoon salt, plus additional as needed

Directions:

1. In a mesh sieve, drain the cashews and rinse well.
2. Combine in a blender the cashews, water, lemon juice, and lemon zest. Blend until smooth and creamy.
3. Add the dill and salt then blend again.
4. Taste and adjust the seasoning if needed.
5. Refrigerate for an hour. The cream will thicken in the refrigerator.

Nutrition Info:

- Info Per Serving: Calories: 38 ;Fat: 3g ;Protein: 1g ;Carbs: 2g .

Garlicky Sauce With Tahini

Servings: 1
Cooking Time: 0 Minutes
Ingredients:

- ½ cup tahini
- 1 garlic clove, minced
- Juice of 1 lemon
- Zest of 1 lemon
- ½ teaspoon salt, plus additional as needed
- ½ cup warm water, plus additional as needed

Directions:

1. Stir together in a small bowl the tahini and garlic.
2. Add the lemon juice, lemon zest, and salt. Stir well.
3. Whisk in ½ cup of warm water, until fully mixed and creamy. Add more water if the sauce is too thick.
4. Taste and adjust the seasoning if needed.
5. Refrigerate in a sealed container.

Nutrition Info:

- Info Per Serving: Calories: 180 ;Fat: 16g ;Protein: 5g ;Carbs: 7g .

Fresh Maple Dressing

Servings: 1 ¼
Cooking Time: 0 Minutes
Ingredients:

- 1 cup canned coconut milk, full-fat
- 2 tablespoons pure maple syrup
- 1 tablespoon Dijon mustard
- 1 tablespoon apple cider vinegar
- Sea salt

Directions:

1. Whisk the coconut milk, maple syrup, mustard, and cider vinegar in a medium bowl until smoothly blended. Season with sea salt.
2. Refrigerate the dressing in a sealed container for up to 1 week.

Nutrition Info:

- Info Per Serving: Calories: 67 ;Fat: 6g ;Protein: 1g;Carbs: 4g.

Awesome Multi-purpose Cream Sauce

Servings: 3 ½
Cooking Time: 12 Minutes
Ingredients:

- 3 cups cubed butternut squash
- ½ cup cashews, soaked in water for 4 hours, drained
- ½ cup water, plus additional for cooking and thinning
- 1 teaspoon salt, plus additional as needed

Directions:

1. Fill a large pot with 2 inches of water and insert a steamer basket. Bring to a boil over high heat.
2. Add the butternut squash to the basket. Cover and steam for 10 to 12 minutes or until tender.
3. Remove from the heat and cool slightly.
4. Transfer the squash to a blender. Add the cashews, ½ cup of water, and salt. Blend until smooth and creamy. Add more water depending on the consistency to thin if necessary.
5. Taste and adjust the seasoning if needed.

Nutrition Info:

- Info Per Serving: Calories: 73 ;Fat: 5g ;Protein: 2g ;Carbs: 8g .

Must-have Ranch Dressing

Servings: 1 ½
Cooking Time: 0 Minutes
Ingredients:

- ½ cup water, filtered
- ½ cup coconut milk, full-fat
- ½ cup hemp seeds, shelled
- 2 tablespoons red wine vinegar
- 1 tablespoon coconut aminos
- 1 tablespoon Dijon mustard
- 2 teaspoons dill weed, dried
- 1 teaspoon parsley, dried
- 1 teaspoon Himalayan salt, fine
- 1 teaspoon fish sauce
- 1 teaspoon garlic powder
- 1 teaspoon onion powder
- 1 teaspoon black pepper, ground

Directions:

1. Place all of the ingredients in a blender and blend until smooth.
2. Store in an airtight glass or ceramic container in the fridge for up to 10 days. Before using, set out at room temperature to soften for a few minutes and shake or stir to mix well.

Nutrition Info:

- Info Per Serving: Calories: 225 ;Fat: 18g ;Protein: 11g;Carbs: 4g.

Dairy Free Apple Cider Vinegar With Tangy Barbecue Sauce

Servings: 2
Cooking Time: 3 To 4 Hours
Ingredients:

- 1¼ cups all-natural ketchup
- ¼ cup molasses
- ¼ cup coconut sugar
- 3 tablespoons apple cider vinegar
- 1 tablespoon Worcestershire sauce
- 1½ teaspoons garlic powder
- 1 teaspoon Dijon mustard
- ½ teaspoon sea salt
- ½ teaspoon onion powder
- Pinch cayenne pepper

Directions:
1. Combine the ketchup, molasses, coconut sugar, vinegar, Worcestershire sauce, garlic powder, mustard, salt, onion powder, and cayenne in your slow cooker.
2. Cover the cooker and set it to low. Cook for 3 to 4 hours.
3. Let cool and refrigerate in an airtight container.

Nutrition Info:
- Info Per Serving: Calories: 416 ;Fat: 15g;Protein: 46g;Carbs: 105g .

Game Changer Pickled Red Onions

Servings: 4
Cooking Time: 10 Minutes
Ingredients:

- 2 cups water, filtered
- 1 cup apple cider vinegar
- 1 teaspoon Himalayan salt, fine
- 1 teaspoon granulated erythritol or another low-carb sweetener
- 2 bay leaves
- 2 red onions, thinly sliced and cut into half-moons

Directions:
1. Combine the water, vinegar, salt, erythritol, and bay leaves in a small saucepan over medium heat. Bring to a light simmer and cook for 8 minutes. Stir to make sure the salt and sweetener have dissolved.
2. In a jar, put all the onion slices with the bay leaves and then pour the hot brine over the onions until fully submerged. Let the onions steep for 30 minutes at room temperature before using. Seal the jar and store it in the fridge for up to a month.

Nutrition Info:
- Info Per Serving: Calories: 5 ;Fat: 7g ;Protein: 6g;Carbs: 2g

To Die For Homemade Mayonnaise

Servings: 1
Cooking Time: 0 Minutes
Ingredients:

- 3 tablespoons coconut vinegar
- 1 teaspoon thyme leaves, dried
- ½ teaspoon garlic, granulated
- ½ teaspoon mustard, dry
- ½ teaspoon Himalayan salt, fine
- 3 large egg yolks
- 1 cup avocado oil

Directions:

1. Place the vinegar and seasonings in a 16 ounces measuring cup or quart-sized mason jar. Add gently the egg yolks and the avocado oil.
2. Insert the immersion blender into the mixture and turn it on high then move it up and down slightly until the mix is completely emulsified. Scrape all of the mayonnaise off of the blender by using a spatula and then transfer the mayonnaise to a jar or other container with a tight-fitting lid.
3. Store in the refrigerator for up to 10 days.

Nutrition Info:

- Info Per Serving: Calories: 262 ;Fat: 30g ;Protein: 1g;Carbs: 4g.

Full Of Spice And Zesty Rub

Servings: ½
Cooking Time: 0 Minutes
Ingredients:

- 1 tablespoon turmeric, ground
- 1 tablespoon ginger, ground
- 1 tablespoon fennel seed, ground
- 1 tablespoon coconut sugar
- 2 teaspoons salt
- 2 teaspoons onion powder
- 1 teaspoon garlic powder
- 1 teaspoon paprika
- ½ teaspoon black pepper, freshly ground

Directions:

1. Combine in a small bowl all the ingredients and mix well.
2. Store in an airtight container for up to 12 months.

Nutrition Info:

- Info Per Serving: Calories: 20 ;Fat: 15g;Protein: 1g ;Carbs: 5g .

Nutritional Sauce With Tofu And Basil

Servings: 2
Cooking Time: 0 Minutes
Ingredients:

- 1 package silken tofu, 12 ounces
- ½ cup fresh basil, chopped
- 2 garlic cloves, lightly crushed
- ½ cup almond butter
- 1 tablespoon lemon juice, fresh
- 1 teaspoon salt
- ¼ teaspoon black pepper, freshly ground

Directions:

1. Combine the tofu, basil, garlic, almond butter, lemon juice, salt, and pepper in a blender or food processor then process until smooth. Thin with a bit of water if too thick.
2. Refrigerate in an airtight container for up to 5 days.

Nutrition Info:

- Info Per Serving: Calories: 120 ;Fat: 10g ;Protein: 6g ;Carbs: 5g .

Delicious Pesto With Kale

Servings: 1
Cooking Time: 0 Minutes
Ingredients:

- 2 cups chopped kale leaves, thoroughly washed and stemmed
- ½ cup almonds, toasted
- 2 garlic cloves
- 3 tablespoons lemon juice, freshly squeezed
- 3 tablespoons extra-virgin olive oil
- 2 teaspoons lemon zest
- 1 teaspoon salt
- ½ teaspoon black pepper, freshly ground
- ¼ teaspoon red pepper flakes

Directions:

1. Combine in a food processor the kale, almonds, garlic, lemon juice, olive oil, lemon zest, salt, black pepper, and red pepper flakes then process until smooth.
2. Refrigerate in an airtight container for up to one week.

Nutrition Info:

- Info Per Serving: Calories: 91 ;Fat: 8g ;Protein: 2g;Carbs: 4g .

Vegan Sauce With Honey, Mustard, And Sesame

Servings: 1
Cooking Time: 0 Minutes
Ingredients:

- ½ cup Dijon mustard
- ½ cup raw honey or maple syrup
- 1 garlic clove, minced
- 1 teaspoon sesame oil, toasted

Directions:

1. Whisk together the Dijon, honey, garlic, and sesame oil in a small bowl.
2. Refrigerate in an airtight container.

Nutrition Info:

- Info Per Serving: Calories: 67 ;Fat: 1g ;Protein: 1g ;Carbs: 14g .

Buttery Slow Cooked Ghee

Servings: 2
Cooking Time: 2 Hours
Ingredients:
- 1 pound unsalted butter, 4 sticks

Directions:
1. Add the butter in the slow cooker. Set the slow cooker to high and leave it uncovered.
2. White foam should appear in 45 minutes. Over time, from 1 to 2 hours, the foam will turn golden brown and give off a nutty smell.
3. Turn off the slow cooker once the foam has turned brown.
4. Line a strainer with a triple thickness of cheesecloth and place the strainer over a wide-mouth jar.
5. Skim off as much of the brown foam as possible using a large spoon or ladle and discard it. Carefully ladle the remaining ghee into the cheesecloth-lined strainer.
6. Discard the cheesecloth once all the ghee has been strained and let the ghee come to room temperature before covering the jar with an airtight lid and refrigerating it. It will last for three months.

Nutrition Info:
- Info Per Serving: Calories: 102 ;Fat: 12g ;Protein: 46g;Carbs: 4g.

Gluten Free Apple Chutney

Servings: 2
Cooking Time: 10 Minutes
Ingredients:

- 1 tablespoon almond oil
- 4 apples, peeled, cored, and diced
- 1 small onion, diced
- ½ cup white raisins
- 1 tablespoon apple cider vinegar
- 1 tablespoon honey
- 1 teaspoon cinnamon, ground
- ½ teaspoon cardamom, ground
- ½ teaspoon ginger, ground
- ½ teaspoon salt

Directions:
1. Heat in a medium saucepan the oil over low heat.
2. Add the apples, onion, raisins6, vinegar, honey, cinnamon, cardamom, ginger, and salt. Cook briefly until the apples release their juices. Bring to a simmer, cover, and cook until the apples are tender for 5 to 10 minutes.
3. Allow to cool completely before serving.

Nutrition Info:
- Info Per Serving: Calories: 120 ;Fat: 2g ;Protein: 1g ;Carbs: 24g .

Natural Dressing With Ginger And Turmeric

Servings: ½
Cooking Time: 0 Minutes
Ingredients:
- 1 cup extra-virgin olive oil
- ¼ cup apple cider vinegar
- ½ teaspoon Dijon mustard
- 1 garlic clove, sliced
- ½ teaspoon fresh ginger root, minced
- 1 teaspoon salt
- ½ teaspoon turmeric, ground
- ¼ teaspoon coriander, ground
- ¼ teaspoon black pepper, freshly ground

Directions:
1. Combine all the ingredients in a blender or food processor and process until smooth.
2. Refrigerate in an airtight container for up to a week.

Nutrition Info:
- Info Per Serving: Calories: 160 ;Fat: 18g; Protein: 46g;Carbs: 4g.

Marinated Greek Dressing

Servings: 1 ½
Cooking Time: 0 Minutes
Ingredients:

- 3 cloves garlic, minced
- 1 cup extra-virgin olive oil or avocado oil
- Juice of 3 lemons, ½ cup
- 2 tablespoons fresh oregano leaves, minced
- 1 teaspoon black pepper, ground
- 1 teaspoon onion powder
- ½ teaspoon Himalayan salt, fine

Directions:

1. In a blender, place all of the ingredients and blend on medium speed until the dressing has emulsified and has a light-brown appearance and the garlic is almost smooth.
2. Store in an airtight container in the fridge for up to 10 days. Shake or stir before using since this. dressing separates very quickly

Nutrition Info:

- Info Per Serving: Calories: 150 ;Fat: 17g ;Protein: 46g;Carbs: 1g .

Tricky Cheesy Yellow Sauce

Servings: 2
Cooking Time: 0 Minutes
Ingredients:

- 1½ cups steamed, mashed cauliflower florets and hot
- ½ cup coconut milk, full-fat
- ½ cup nutritional yeast
- 1 tablespoon unsalted butter, ghee, or lard
- 1½ teaspoons coconut vinegar
- 1 teaspoon Himalayan salt, fine
- 1 teaspoon garlic powder

Directions:

1. Place all of the ingredients in a blender. Cover and blend on low, slowly bringing the speed up to high.
2. Continue to blend until the sauce is completely smooth. Taste for seasoning and add a little more salt and/or garlic powder if you like.
3. Store in an airtight container in the refrigerator for up to a week. Warm in a saucepan on the stovetop over medium heat and stir occasionally.

Nutrition Info:

- Info Per Serving: Calories: 185 ;Fat: 11g ;Protein: 11g;Carbs: 15g .

Soups & Stews

Fennel & Parsnip Bisque

Servings: 6
Cooking Time: 30 Minutes
Ingredients:

- 1 tbsp extra-virgin olive oil
- 2 green onions, chopped
- ½ fennel bulb, sliced
- 2 large carrots, shredded
- 2 parsnips, shredded
- 1 turnip, chopped
- 2 garlic cloves, minced
- ½ tsp dried thyme
- ¼ tsp dried marjoram
- 6 cups vegetable broth
- 1 cup plain soy milk
- 1 tbsp minced fresh parsley

Directions:

1. Heat the oil in a pot over medium heat. Place in green onions, fennel, carrots, parsnips, turnip, and garlic. Sauté for 5 minutes until softened. Add in thyme, marjoram, and broth. Bring to a boil, lower the heat, and simmer for 20 minutes. Transfer to a blender and pulse the soup until smooth. Mix in soy milk. Top with parsley to serve.

Nutrition Info:

- Info Per Serving: Calories: 115;Fat: 3g;Protein: 2g;Carbs: 20g.

Spicy Turkey Soup

Servings: 4
Cooking Time: 35 Minutes
Ingredients:

- 1 can fire-roasted tomatoes with their juice
- 2 tbsp extra-virgin olive oil
- 1 lb ground turkey
- 1 zucchini, sliced
- 1 shallot, chopped
- 2 garlic cloves, minced
- Sea salt and pepper to taste
- 1 Bird's eye chili, minced
- ½ tsp ground cumin
- 1 can black beans
- 4 cups chicken broth
- 2 tbsp chopped scallions
- 2 tbsp chopped cilantro

Directions:

1. Warm the olive oil in a pot over medium heat. Add the ground turkey and cook for 5 minutes until no longer pink. Add the zucchini, shallot, chili, garlic, cumin, salt, and pepper and cook for 5 minutes until tender. Put in the black beans, tomatoes, and chicken broth and bring to a boil. Low the heat and simmer for 10 minutes. Garnish with scallions and cilantro. Serve immediately.

Nutrition Info:

- Info Per Serving: Calories: 380;Fat: 15g;Protein: 29g;Carbs: 34g.

Green Bean & Zucchini Velouté

Servings: 6
Cooking Time: 30 Minutes
Ingredients:

- 2 tbsp minced jarred pimiento
- 3 tbsp extra-virgin olive oil
- 1 onion, chopped
- 1 garlic clove, minced
- 2 cups green beans
- 4 cups vegetable broth
- 3 medium zucchini, sliced
- ½ tsp dried marjoram
- ½ cup plain almond milk

Directions:

1. Heat oil in a pot and sauté onion and garlic for 5 minutes. Add in green beans and broth. Cook for 10 minutes. Stir in zucchini and cook for 10 minutes. Transfer to a food processor and pulse until smooth. Return to the pot and mix in almond milk; cook until hot. Top with pimiento.

Nutrition Info:

- Info Per Serving: Calories: 95;Fat: 7g;Protein: 2g;Carbs: 8g.

Pumpkin & Garbanzo Chili With Kale

Servings: 6
Cooking Time: 60 Minutes
Ingredients:

- 1 cup garbanzo beans, soaked
- 1 can diced tomatoes
- 2 cups chopped pumpkin
- 6 cups water
- 2 tbsp chili powder
- 1 tsp onion powder
- ½ tsp garlic powder
- 3 cups kale, chopped
- ½ tsp sea salt

Directions:

1. In a saucepan over medium heat, add garbanzo, tomatoes, pumpkin, 2 cups water, salt, chili, onion, and garlic powders. Bring to a boil. Reduce the heat and simmer for 50 minutes. Stir in kale and cook for 5 minutes. Serve.

Nutrition Info:

- Info Per Serving: Calories: 165;Fat: 2g;Protein: 19g;Carbs: 31g.

Super Simple Stew With Mango And Black Bean

Servings: 4
Cooking Time: 10 Minutes
Ingredients:

- 2 tablespoons coconut oil
- 1 onion, chopped
- 2 pieces of 15 ounces cans black beans, drained and rinsed
- 1 tablespoon chili powder
- 1 teaspoon salt
- ¼ teaspoon black pepper, freshly ground
- 1 cup water
- 2 ripe mangos, sliced thin
- ¼ cup chopped fresh cilantro, divided
- ¼ cup sliced scallions, divided

Directions:

1. Melt the coconut oil in a large pot over high heat.
2. Add the onion and sauté for 5 minutes.
3. Add the black beans, chili powder, salt, pepper, and water. Bring to a boil. Reduce the heat to simmer and cook for 5 minutes.
4. Remove the pot from the heat; stir in the mangos just before serving. Garnish each serving with cilantro and scallions.

Nutrition Info:

- Info Per Serving: Calories: 431 ; Fat: 9g ;Protein: 20g ;Carbs: 72g .

Classic Soup With Butternut Squash

Servings: 6
Cooking Time: 30 Minutes
Ingredients:

- 1 onion, chopped roughly
- 4½ cups plus 2 tablespoons water, divided
- 1 large butternut squash, washed, peeled, ends trimmed, halved, seeded, and cut into ½-inch chunks
- 2 celery stalks, chopped roughly
- 3 carrots, peeled and chopped roughly
- 1 teaspoon sea salt, plus additional as needed

Directions:

1. Sauté the onion in 2 tablespoons of water in a large pot set over medium heat for about 5 minutes, or until soft.
2. Add the squash, celery, carrot, and salt. Bring to a boil.
3. Reduce the heat to low, Cover, and simmer for 25 minutes.
4. Purée the soup in a blender until smooth, working in batches if necessary and taking care of the hot liquid. Taste, and adjust the seasoning if necessary.

Nutrition Info:

- Info Per Serving: Calories: 104 ;Fat: 15g;Protein: 2g ;Carbs: 27g .

Garlic Veggie Bisque

Servings: 6
Cooking Time: 25 Minutes
Ingredients:

- 1 red onion, chopped
- 2 carrots, chopped
- 1 zucchini, sliced
- 1 ripe tomato, quartered
- 2 garlic cloves, crushed
- 3 tbsp extra-virgin olive oil
- ½ tsp dried rosemary
- Sea salt and pepper to taste
- 6 cups vegetable broth
- 1 tbsp minced fresh parsley

Directions:

1. Preheat your oven to 400°F. Arrange the onion, carrots, zucchini, tomato, and garlic on a greased baking dish. Sprinkle with oil, rosemary, salt, and pepper. Cover with foil and roast for 30 minutes. Uncover and turn them. Roast for another 10 minutes. Transfer the veggies into a pot and pour in the broth. Bring to a boil, lower the heat and simmer for 5 minutes. Transfer to a food processor and blend the soup until smooth. Return to the pot and cook until hot. Serve topped with parsley.

Nutrition Info:

- Info Per Serving: Calories: 95;Fat: 7g;Protein: 1g;Carbs: 8g.

Moroccan Inspired Lentil Soup

Servings: 2
Cooking Time: 40 Minutes
Ingredients:
- 2 tablespoon extra-virgin olive oil
- 1 yellow onion, diced
- 1 carrot, diced
- 1 clove of minced garlic, diced
- 1 teaspoon cumin, ground
- ½ teaspoon ginger, ground
- 2 tablespoon low-fat Greek yogurt
- ½ teaspoon turmeric, ground
- ½ teaspoon red chili flakes
- 1 can tomatoes, chopped
- 1 cup dried yellow lentils, soaked
- 5 cups of low salt vegetable stock or homemade chicken stock
- 1 lemon

Directions:
1. Heat the oil in a large pan on medium-high heat.
2. Sauté the onion and carrot for 5 to 6 minutes until softened and starting to brown.
3. Add the garlic, ginger, chili flakes, cumin, and turmeric, cook for 2 minutes.
4. Add the tomatoes, scraping any brown bits from the bottom of the pan, and cooking until the liquid is reduced for 15 to 20 minutes).
5. Add the lentils and stock and turn the heat up to reach a boil before lowering the heat, covering, and for 10 minutes, simmer.
6. Serve with a wedge of lemon on the side and a dollop of Greek yogurt.

Nutrition Info:
- Info Per Serving: Calories: 1048 ;Fat: 53g ;Protein: 19g Carbs: 128g .

Easy Garbanzo Soup

Servings: 4
Cooking Time: 25 Minutes
Ingredients:
- 2 tbsp extra-virgin olive oil
- 1 onion, chopped
- 1 green bell pepper, diced
- 1 carrot, peeled and diced
- 4 garlic cloves, minced
- 1 can garbanzo beans
- 1 cup spinach, chopped
- 4 cups vegetable stock
- ¼ tsp ground cumin
- Sea salt to taste

Directions:
1. Heat the oil in a pot over medium heat. Place in onion, garlic, bell pepper, and carrot and sauté for 5 minutes until tender. Stir in garbanzo beans, spinach, stock, cumin, and salt. Cook for 10 minutes. Mash the garbanzo using a potato masher, leaving some chunks. Serve.

Nutrition Info:
- Info Per Serving: Calories: 120;Fat: 7g;Protein: 2g;Carbs: 13g.

Roasted Basil & Tomato Soup

Servings: 4
Cooking Time: 60 Minutes
Ingredients:

- 2 lb tomatoes, halved
- 2 tsp garlic powder
- 3 tbsp extra-virgin olive oil
- 1 tbsp balsamic vinegar
- Sea salt and pepper to taste
- 4 shallots, chopped
- 2 cups vegetable broth
- ½ cup basil leaves, chopped

Directions:

1. Preheat your oven to 450°F. Mix tomatoes, garlic, 2 tbsp of oil, vinegar, salt, and pepper in a bowl. Arrange the tomatoes onto a baking dish. Sprinkle with some olive oil, garlic powder, balsamic vinegar, salt, and pepper. Bake for 30 minutes until the tomatoes get dark brown color. Take out from the oven; reserve.

2. Heat the remaining oil in a pot over medium heat. Place the shallots and cook for 3 minutes, stirring often. Add in roasted tomatoes and broth. Bring to a boil, then lower the heat and simmer for 10 minutes. Blitz the soup in a food processor until smooth. Serve topped with basil.

Nutrition Info:

- Info Per Serving: Calories: 155;Fat: 11g;Protein: 5g;Carbs: 14g.

Mixed Mushroom Soup

Servings: 4
Cooking Time: 40 Minutes
Ingredients:

- 5 oz button mushrooms, chopped
- ½ cup cremini mushrooms, chopped
- ½ cup shiitake mushrooms, chopped
- 1 vegetable stock cube, crushed
- 2 tbsp extra-virgin olive oil
- 1 onion, finely chopped
- 1 clove garlic, minced
- ½ lb celery root, chopped
- ½ tsp dried rosemary
- 1 tbsp plain vinegar
- 1 cup coconut cream
- 4 leaves basil, chopped

Directions:

1. Place a saucepan over medium heat, warm the olive oil, then sauté the onion, garlic, mushrooms, and celery root until golden brown and fragrant, about 6 minutes. Fetch out some mushrooms and reserve for garnishing. Add the rosemary, 3 cups of water, stock cube, and vinegar. Stir the mixture and bring it to a boil for 6 minutes. After, reduce the heat and simmer the soup for 15 minutes or until the celery is soft. Mix in the coconut cream and puree the ingredients using an immersion blender. Simmer for 2 minutes. Spoon the soup into serving bowls, garnish with the reserved mushrooms and basil. Serve.

Nutrition Info:

- Info Per Serving: Calories: 290;Fat: 28g;Protein: 7g;Carbs: 9g.

Asian-style Bean Soup

Servings: 4
Cooking Time: 55 Minutes
Ingredients:

- 1 cup canned white beans
- 2 tsp olive oil
- 1 red onion, diced
- 1 tbsp minced fresh ginger
- 2 cubed sweet potatoes
- 1 cup sliced zucchini
- Sea salt and pepper to taste
- 4 cups vegetable stock
- 1 bunch spinach, chopped
- Toasted sesame seeds

Directions:

1. Warm the oil in a pot over medium heat. Place the onion and ginger and cook for 5 minutes until soft. Add in sweet potatoes and cook for 10 minutes. Put in zucchini and cook for 5 minutes. Season with pepper and salt. Pour in the stock and bring to a boil. Simmer for 25 minutes. Stir in beans and spinach. Cook until the spinach wilts, 5 minutes. Garnish with sesame seeds. Serve and enjoy!

Nutrition Info:

- Info Per Serving: Calories: 150;Fat: 4g;Protein: 7g;Carbs: 25g.

Chicken & Vegetable Stew With Barley

Servings: 6
Cooking Time: 30 Minutes
Ingredients:

- 1 lb chicken breasts, cubed
- 3 tbsp extra-virgin olive oil
- 1 onion, chopped
- 2 garlic cloves, minced
- 2 turnips, chopped
- 1 cup pearl barley
- 1 can diced tomatoes
- 3 tsp dried mixed herbs
- Sea salt and pepper to taste

Directions:

1. Warm the olive oil in a pot over medium heat. Add the chicken, onion, and garlic and sauté for 6-8 minutes. Stir in the turnips, barley, tomatoes, 3 cups of water, and herbs. Cook for 20 minutes. Adjust the seasoning. Serve.

Nutrition Info:

- Info Per Serving: Calories: 350;Fat: 15g;Protein: 21g;Carbs: 36g.

French Peasant Turkey Stew

Servings: 4
Cooking Time: 40 Minutes
Ingredients:

- 2 cups leftover roast turkey, shredded
- 2 sweet potatoes, cut into quarters
- 2 cups baby carrots
- 1 cup sliced mushrooms
- 1 jar chicken gravy
- 2 cups chicken broth
- 1 tsp dried rosemary
- ½ cup frozen green peas

Directions:

1. Add the sweet potatoes, baby carrots, mushrooms, chicken gravy, broth, and rosemary to a medium pot over medium heat. Bring to a boil, reduce the heat and simmer covered 20 minutes, stirring occasionally, or until vegetables are tender. Stir in turkey and peas. Simmer for another 5 minutes until heated through. Serve and enjoy!

Nutrition Info:

- Info Per Serving: Calories: 285;Fat: 10g;Protein: 28g;Carbs: 21.8g.

Chicken & Ginger Soup

Servings: 4
Cooking Time: 20 Minutes
Ingredients:

- 2 cups skinless leftover roasted chicken, diced
- 4 cups no-salt-added chicken broth
- 1 carrot, chopped
- 2 tbsp extra-virgin olive oil
- 1 onion, chopped
- 1 red bell pepper, chopped
- 1 tbsp grated fresh ginger
- Sea salt and pepper to taste

Directions:

1. Warm the olive oil in a pot over medium heat and add the onion, red bell peppers, carrot, and ginger. Sauté for 5 minutes until the veggies are soft. Mix in chicken, chicken broth, salt, and pepper. Bring to a boil, reduce the heat, and simmer for 5 minutes. Serve immediately.

Nutrition Info:

- Info Per Serving: Calories: 340;Fat: 16g;Protein: 7g;Carbs: 12g.

Curry Soup With Butternut Squash And Coconut

Servings: 4 To 6
Cooking Time: 4 Hours
Ingredients:

- 2 tablespoons coconut oil
- 1 pound butternut squash, peeled and cut into 1-inch cubes
- 1 small head cauliflower, cut into 1-inch pieces
- 1 onion, sliced
- 1 tablespoon curry powder
- ½ cup no-added-sugar apple juice
- 4 cups vegetable broth
- 1 can coconut milk, 13 ½ ounces
- 1 teaspoon salt
- ¼ teaspoon white pepper, freshly ground
- ¼ cup chopped fresh cilantro, divided

Directions:

1. Combine the coconut oil, butternut squash, cauliflower, onion, curry powder, apple juice, vegetable broth, coconut milk, salt, and white pepper in the slower cooker. Set on high for 4 hours.
2. Before serving, purée it in a blender.
3. Garnish with cilantro.

Nutrition Info:

- Info Per Serving: Calories: 416 ;Fat: 31g ;Protein: 10g ;Carbs: 30g .

Roasted-pumpkin Soup

Servings: 4
Cooking Time: 55 Minutes
Ingredients:
- 2 red onions, cut into wedges
- 2 garlic cloves, skinned
- 10 oz pumpkin, cubed
- 4 tbsp extra-virgin olive oil
- Juice of 1 lime
- 1 tbsp toasted pumpkin seeds

Directions:
1. Preheat your oven to 400°F. Place onions, garlic, and pumpkin on a baking sheet and drizzle with some olive oil. Season with salt and pepper. Roast for 30 minutes or until the vegetables are golden brown and fragrant. Remove the vegetables from the oven and transfer to a pot. Add 2 cups of water, bring the ingredients to boil over medium heat for 15 minutes. Turn the heat off. Add the remaining olive oil and puree until smooth. Stir in lime juice. Spoon into serving bowls. Garnish with pumpkin seeds. Serve and enjoy!

Nutrition Info:
- Info Per Serving: Calories: 210;Fat: 16g;Protein: 22g;Carbs: 17g.

Healthy Soup With Turmeric And Broccoli

Servings: 4 To 6
Cooking Time: 3 To 4 Hours
Ingredients:
- 2 medium heads broccoli
- ½ medium onion, diced
- 1 tablespoon extra-virgin olive oil
- 1 tablespoon turmeric, ground
- ½ teaspoon garlic powder
- ½ teaspoon ginger, ground
- 1 teaspoon lemon juice, freshly squeezed
- ½ teaspoon sea salt
- 4 cups vegetable broth
- Freshly ground black pepper

Directions:
1. Combine the broccoli, onion, olive oil, turmeric, garlic powder, ginger, lemon juice, salt, and broth in your slow cooker and season with pepper.
2. Cover the cooker and set it to low. Cook for 3 to 4 hours and serve.

Nutrition Info:
- Info Per Serving: Calories: 144 ;Fat: 5g ;Protein: 9g ;Carbs: 22g .

Classic Vegetarian Tagine

Servings: 2
Cooking Time: 45 Minutes
Ingredients:

- 2 tablespoon coconut oil
- 1 onion, diced
- 1 parsnip, peeled and diced
- 2 cloves of garlic
- 1 teaspoon cumin, ground
- ½ teaspoon ginger, ground
- ½ teaspoon cinnamon, ground
- ¼ teaspoon cayenne pepper
- 3 tablespoon tomato paste
- 1 sweet potato, peeled & diced
- 1 purple potato, peeled & diced
- 4 baby carrots, peeled & diced
- 4 cups low-salt vegetable stock
- 2 cups kale leaves
- 2 tablespoons lemon juice
- ¼ cup cilantro, roughly chopped
- handful of almonds, toasted

Directions:

1. Heat the oil in a large pot on a medium-high heat before sautéing the onion until soft.
2. Add the parsnip for 10 minutes or until golden brown.
3. Add the garlic, cumin, ginger, cinnamon, tomato paste, and cayenne.
4. For 2 minutes, cook until it has a lovely scent.
5. Fold in the sweet potatoes, carrots, and purple potatoes and stock and then bring to a boil.
6. Turn heat down and simmer for 20 minutes.
7. Add in the kale and lemon juice, simmering for 2 minutes more or until the leaves are slightly wilted.
8. Garnish with cilantro and the nuts to serve.

Nutrition Info:

- Info Per Serving: Calories: 1115 ;Fat: 51g ;Protein: 19g ;Carbs: 150g .

Peppery Soup With Tomato

Servings: 2
Cooking Time: 35 Minutes
Ingredients:

- 2 red bell peppers
- 4 beef tomatoes
- 1 sweet onion, chopped
- 1 garlic clove, chopped
- 3 cups homemade chicken broth
- 2 habanero chilis, stems removed and chopped
- 2 tablespoon extra-virgin olive oil

Directions:

1. Preheat the broiler to medium-high heat and grill the bell peppers, turning halfway for 10 minutes until the skins are blackened.
2. Heat water in a pan on medium to high heat and cut a small x at the bottom of each tomato using a sharp knife.
3. Transfer to separate dish pepper once cooked and cover.
4. For 20 seconds, blanch the tomatoes in simmering water.
5. Remove and plunge into ice-cold water.
6. Peel and chop tomatoes, reserving the juices.
7. Sauté the onion, garlic, chili, and 2 tablespoons of oil in a saucepan on medium-high heat, stirring for 8-10 minutes until golden.
8. Add the tomatoes with the juices, the peppers, and broth to the onions and cover and simmer for 10-15 minutes or until heated through.
9. Purée in a blender and serve.

Nutrition Info:

- Info Per Serving: Calories: 741| Fat: 32g ;Protein: 82g ;Carbs: 30g .

Desserts

Chocolate Fudge With Nuts

Servings: 4
Cooking Time: 10 Minutes + Cooling Time
Ingredients:

- 3 cups chocolate chips
- ¼ cup thick coconut milk
- 1 ½ tsp vanilla extract
- A pinch of sea salt
- 1 cup chopped mixed nuts

Directions:

1. Line a square pan with baking paper. Melt the chocolate chips, coconut milk, and vanilla in a medium pot over low heat. Mix in the salt and nuts until well distributed and pour the mixture into the square pan. Refrigerate for at least 2 hours. Cut into squares and serve.

Nutrition Info:

- Info Per Serving: Calories: 905;Fat: 32g;Protein: 8g;Carbs: 152g.

Delicious Nutmeg Muffins With Vanilla And Blueberries

Servings: 4
Cooking Time: 20 Minutes
Ingredients:

- 3 free range egg whites
- 1/10 cup chickpea flour
- 1 tablespoon coconut flour
- 1 teaspoon baking powder
- 1 tablespoon nutmeg, grated
- 1 teaspoon vanilla extract
- 1 teaspoon stevia
- ½ cup fresh blueberries

Directions:

1. Preheat the oven to 325°F.
2. In a mixing bowl, mix all of the ingredients.
3. Divide the batter into 4 and spoon into a muffin tin.
4. Bake in the oven for 15 to 20 minutes or until cooked through.
5. Your knife should pull out clean from the middle of the muffins once done.
6. Allow to cool on a wire rack before serving.

Nutrition Info:

- Info Per Serving: Calories: 63 ;Fat: 1g ;Protein: 4g ;Carbs: 10g .

Timeless Fruit Cocktail And Rose Water Yogurt

Servings: 4
Cooking Time: 0 Minutes
Ingredients:

- 2 cups fresh strawberries, halved
- 2 plums, pitted and cubed
- 2 kiwis, peeled and cubed
- 1 peach, peeled and cubed
- 1 cup honeydew melon, peeled and cubed
- 1 cup of tart cherries, pitted and halved
- 1 cup grapes, halved
- 1 cup fresh pineapple, cubed
- 2 cups low-fat Greek yogurt

Directions:

1. Add all of the fruit to a mixing bowl and stir.
2. Add rose water to yogurt and stir in a separate bowl.
3. Divide fruit into 4 servings and top with rose water yogurt.
4. Enjoy.

Nutrition Info:

- Info Per Serving: Calories: 222 ;Fat: 2g ;Protein: 8g ;Carbs: 46g .

Almond & Chocolate Cookies

Servings: 6
Cooking Time: 20 Minutes
Ingredients:

- ¼ cup cocoa powder
- ¾ cup almond butter, softened
- ½ cup coconut sugar
- 1 egg
- 1 egg yolk
- 2 tsp vanilla extract
- ½ cup dark chocolate chips,
- 1 tsp baking soda
- ¼ tsp salt

Directions:

1. Preheat the oven to 350°F. Line two baking sheets with parchment paper. Combine the cocoa powder, almond butter, vanilla extract, and coconut sugar in a bowl. In another bowl, beat the egg and egg yolk, pour it into the almond mixture, and stir. Mix in baking soda, salt, and chocolate chips. Shape 12 balls out of the mixture and place 6 of them on each sheet and bake for 9-10 minutes. Let rest for 5 minutes and sprinkle with salt. Serve cold.

Nutrition Info:

- Info Per Serving: Calories: 225;Fat: 7g;Protein: 6g;Carbs: 22g.

Spiced Chai With Baked Apples

Servings: 5
Cooking Time: 2 To 3 Hours
Ingredients:

- 5 apples
- ½ cup water
- ½ cup pecans, crushed
- ¼ cup coconut oil, melted
- 1 teaspoon cinnamon, ground
- ½ teaspoon ginger, ground
- ¼ teaspoon cardamom, ground
- ¼ teaspoon cloves, ground

Directions:

1. Core each apple and peel off a thin strip from the top of each.
2. Add the water to the slow cooker. Gently place each apple upright along the bottom.
3. Stir together in a small bowl the pecans, coconut oil, cinnamon, ginger, cardamom, and cloves. Drizzle the mixture over the tops of the apples.
4. Cover the cooker and set to high. Cook for 2 to 3 hours until the apples soften then serve.

Nutrition Info:

- Info Per Serving: Calories: 217 ;Fat: 12g ;Protein: 16g;Carbs: 30g .

Lemony Lavender With Strawberry Compote

Servings: 4
Cooking Time: 30 Minutes
Ingredients:
- 2 cups strawberries, halved
- juice and zest a lemon
- 2 tablespoons raw honey
- 1 tablespoon lavender extract

Directions:
1. Into a saucepan, put all of the ingredients together and then simmer on a very low heat until the honey has been dissolved for 15 to 20 minutes.
2. Add the strawberries when the sauce starts to thicken and simmer for 5 to 10 minutes.
3. Serve warm right away or allow to cool and drizzle over yogurt later on.

Nutrition Info:
- Info Per Serving: Calories: 67 ;Fat: 2g;Protein: 1g ;Carbs: 15g .

Sicilian Papaya Sorbet

Servings: 4
Cooking Time: 5 Minutes + Freezing Time
Ingredients:
- 8 cups papaya chunks
- 2 limes, juiced and zested
- ½ cup pure date sugar

Directions:
1. Blend the papaya, lime juice, and sugar in your food processor until smooth. Transfer the mixture to a glass dish. Freeze for 2 hours. Take out from the freezer and scrape the top ice layer with a fork. Back to the freezer for 1 hour. Repeat the process a few more times until all the ice is scraped up. Serve frozen garnished with lime zest strips.

Nutrition Info:
- Info Per Serving: Calories: 250;Fat: 1g;Protein: 2g;Carbs: 64g.

Raisin Oatmeal Biscuits

Servings: 6
Cooking Time: 20 Minutes
Ingredients:
- ½ cup almond butter
- 1 cup date sugar
- ¼ cup pineapple juice
- 1 cup whole-grain flour
- 1 tsp baking powder
- ½ tsp salt
- 1 tsp vanilla extract
- 1 cup old-fashioned oats
- ½ cup dark chocolate chips
- ½ cup raisins

Directions:
1. Preheat your oven to 370ºF. Beat the almond butter and date sugar in a bowl until creamy and fluffy. Pour in the juice and blend. Mix in flour, baking powder, salt, and vanilla. Stir in oats, chocolate chips, and raisins. Spread the dough on a baking sheet and bake for 15 minutes. Let completely cool on a rack. Serve and enjoy!

Nutrition Info:
- Info Per Serving: Calories: 385;Fat: 17g;Protein: 6g;Carbs: 60g.

Coconut Chia Pudding

Servings: 4
Cooking Time: 30 Minutes
Ingredients:

- 1 orange, zested and juiced
- 1 can coconut milk
- 2 pitted dates
- 1 tbsp chia seeds

Directions:

1. In a blender, put the orange juice, orange zest, coconut milk, dates, and chia seeds. Blitz until smooth. Transfer to a bowl and put it in the fridge for 20 minutes. Top with berries, whipped cream, or toasted coconut and serve.

Nutrition Info:

- Info Per Serving: Calories: 30;Fat: 1g;Protein: 1g;Carbs: 7g.

Vanilla Berry Tarts

Servings: 4
Cooking Time: 35 Minutes + Cooling Time
Ingredients:

- 4 eggs, beaten
- 1/3 cup whole-wheat flour
- ½ tsp salt
- ¼ cup almond butter
- 3 tbsp pure malt syrup
- 6 oz coconut cream
- 6 tbsp pure date sugar
- ¾ tsp vanilla extract
- 1 cup mixed frozen berries

Directions:

1. Preheat your oven to 350ºF. In a large bowl, combine flour and salt. Add almond butter and whisk until crumbly. Pour in the eggs and malt syrup and mix until smooth dough forms. Flatten the dough on a flat surface, cover with plastic wrap, and refrigerate for 1 hour.
2. Dust a working surface with some flour, remove the dough onto the surface, and using a rolling pin, flatten the dough into a 1-inch diameter circle. Use a large cookie cutter, cut out rounds of the dough and fit into the pie pans. Use a knife to trim the edges of the pan. Lay a parchment paper on the dough cups, pour on some baking beans, and bake in the oven until golden brown, 15-20 minutes. Remove the pans from the oven, pour out the baking beans, and allow cooling. In a bowl, mix coconut cream, date sugar, and vanilla extract. Divide the mixture into the tart cups and top with berries. Serve.

Nutrition Info:

- Info Per Serving: Calories: 590;Fat: 38g;Protein: 13g;Carbs: 56g.

Impressive Parfait With Yogurt, Berry, And Walnut

Servings: 2
Cooking Time: 0 Minutes
Ingredients:

- 2 cups plain unsweetened yogurt, or plain unsweetened coconut yogurt or almond yogurt
- 2 tablespoons honey
- 1 cup blueberries, fresh
- 1 cup raspberries, fresh
- ½ cup walnut pieces

Directions:

1. Whisk the yogurt and honey in a medium bowl. Spoon into 2 serving bowls.
2. Top each with ½ cup blueberries, ½ cup raspberries, and ¼ cup walnut pieces.

Nutrition Info:

- Info Per Serving: Calories: 505 ;Fat: 22g ;Protein: 23g ;Carbs: 56g .

Cinnamon Tropical Cobbler

Servings: 6
Cooking Time: 45 Minutes
Ingredients:

- 3 apples, shredded
- 2 ripe pineapples, chopped
- 2 tsp lemon juice
- ½ cup pure date sugar
- 2 tbsp arrowroot
- 1 tsp ground cinnamon
- ½ tsp ground allspice
- 1 cup whole-grain flour
- 1 ½ tsp baking powder
- ¼ tsp sea salt
- 2 tbsp peanut butter
- ½ cup soy milk

Directions:

1. Preheat your oven to 390°F. Arrange apples and pineapples on a greased baking pan. Drizzle with lemon juice, arrowroot, cinnamon, and allspice. In a bowl, combine flour, date sugar, baking powder, and salt. Stir in the peanut butter with a fork until the batter resembles crumbs. Mix in soy milk. Spread the mixture over the fruit and bake for 30 minutes. Serve and enjoy!

Nutrition Info:

- Info Per Serving: Calories: 190;Fat: 2g;Protein: 4g;Carbs: 41g.

Oatmeal Chocolate Cookies

Servings: 2
Cooking Time: 30 Minutes
Ingredients:

- ¼ cup whole wheat flour
- ¼ cup oats
- 1 tbsp olive oil
- 2 tbsp packed brown sugar
- ½ tsp vanilla extract
- 1 tbsp honey
- 2 tbsp coconut milk
- 2 tsp coconut oil
- ⅛ tsp sea salt
- 3 tbsp dark chocolate chips

Directions:

1. Combine all of the ingredients in a large bowl. Line a baking pan with parchment paper. Make lemon-sized cookies out of the mixture and flatten them onto the lined pan. Add some water to your Instant Pot and lower the trivet. Add the baking pan to your pot. Cook for 15 minutes on "Manual" on high pressure. Release the pressure quickly, carefully open the lid and serve warm.

Nutrition Info:

- Info Per Serving: Calories: 415;Fat: 20g;Protein: 6g;Carbs: 60g.

Apple & Berry Parfait

Servings: 4
Cooking Time: 15 Minutes
Ingredients:
- 2 tbsp pistachios, chopped
- 1 can coconut milk
- 2 tbsp honey
- 4 cups mixed berries
- 1 peeled apple, chopped

Directions:
1. Put the coconut milk in the refrigerator to chill overnight. The next day, open the tin and scoop the solids have collected on top into a mixing bowl. Set aside the water. Add the honey to the coconut milk and whisk well. Divide half of the mixture between 4 glasses. Top with half of the fruit. Spoon over the remaining coconut mixture and finish with the remaining fruit. Chill the parfaits until needed. Sprinkle with pistachios before serving.

Nutrition Info:
- Info Per Serving: Calories: 390;Fat: 22g;Protein: 10g;Carbs: 47g.

Blueberry & Almond Greek Yogurt

Servings: 4
Cooking Time: 5 Minutes
Ingredients:
- 3 cups plain greek yogurt
- 1 ½ cups blueberries
- ¾ cup almonds, chopped
- ½ cup honey

Directions:
1. Divide the greek yogurt between four bowls and top each with blueberries, almonds, and honey. Serve and enjoy!

Nutrition Info:
- Info Per Serving: Calories: 460;Fat: 19g;Protein: 4g;Carbs: 63g.

Nightshade Free Cinnamon Pecans

Servings: 3 ½
Cooking Time: 3 To 4 Hours
Ingredients:
- 1 tablespoon coconut oil
- 1 large egg white
- 2 tablespoons cinnamon, ground
- 2 teaspoons vanilla extract
- ¼ cup maple syrup
- 2 tablespoons coconut sugar
- ¼ teaspoon sea salt
- 3 cups pecan halves

Directions:
1. Coat the slow cooker with the coconut oil.
2. Whisk the egg white in a medium bowl.
3. Add the cinnamon, vanilla, maple syrup, coconut sugar, and salt. Whisk well to combine.
4. Add the pecans and stir to coat. Pour the pecans into the slow cooker.
5. Cover the cooker and set to low. Cook for 3 to 4 hours.
6. Remove the pecans from the slow cooker and spread them on a baking sheet or other cooling surface. Before serving, let cool for 5 to 10 minutes. Store in an airtight container at room temperature for up to 2 weeks.

Nutrition Info:
- Info Per Serving: Calories: 195 ;Fat: 18g ;Protein: 2g ;Carbs: 9g .

Mid Afternoon Grilled Banana And Homemade Nut Butter

Servings: 2
Cooking Time: 5 Minutes
Ingredients:
- 2 bananas
- 1 cup almonds

Directions:
1. Peel bananas and cut lengthways with a knife down the center to form a banana split.
2. Blend the almonds until smooth to form your own nut butter.
3. Spread almond butter along the middle of the bananas and broil for 3 to 4 minutes on a medium heat until browned.
4. Serve immediately.

Nutrition Info:
- Info Per Serving: Calories: 3 ;Fat: 5g;Protein: 6g;Carbs: 2g

Apple & Cashew Quiche

Servings: 6
Cooking Time: 55 Minutes
Ingredients:
- 5 apples, peeled and sliced
- ½ cup pure maple syrup
- 1 tbsp fresh orange juice
- 1 tsp ground cinnamon
- ½ cup whole-grain flour
- ½ cup old-fashioned oats
- ½ cup chopped cashew
- 2 tbsp pure date sugar
- ½ cup almond butter

Directions:
1. Preheat your oven to 360ºF. Place apples in a greased baking pan. Stir in maple syrup and orange juice. Sprinkle with ½ tsp of cinnamon. In a bowl, combine the flour, oats, cashew, sugar, and remaining cinnamon. Blend in the almond butter until the mixture crumbs. Pour over the apples and bake for 45 minutes. Serve and enjoy!

Nutrition Info:
- Info Per Serving: Calories: 820;Fat: 42g;Protein: 9g;Carbs: 115g.

Almond & Chia Bites With Cherries

Servings: 2
Cooking Time: 20 Minutes
Ingredients:

- 1 cup cherries, pitted
- 1 cup shredded coconut
- ¼ cup chia seeds
- ¾ cup ground almonds
- ¼ cup cocoa nibs

Directions:

1. Blend cherries, coconut, chia seeds, almonds, and cocoa nibs in a food processor until crumbly. Shape the mixture into 24 balls and arrange on a lined baking sheet. Let sit in the fridge for 15 minutes. Serve and enjoy!

Nutrition Info:

- Info Per Serving: Calories: 95;Fat: 2g;Protein: 4g;Carbs: 22g.

Natural Crispy Seasonal Fruits

Servings: 8
Cooking Time: 30 To 40 Minutes
Ingredients:

- 2 cups rolled oats, 200 g
- 1 ½ cups gluten-free flour, 180g
- ¾ cup firmly packed brown sugar, 150g
- ½ teaspoon cinnamon, ground
- ¼ teaspoon nutmeg, ground
- ¼ teaspoon kosher salt
- ½ cup (4 ½ ounces) unsalted butter, cut into 8 pieces
- 2 to 3 pounds apples or pears, peeled, cored, and chopped, or other seasonal fruit
- 1 to 2 teaspoons raw cane sugar
- Greek yogurt
- Honey

Directions:

1. Preheat the oven to 350°F. Line a baking sheet with parchment paper, and place eight 1-cup (240-ml) ramekins on the prepared sheet.
2. In a large bowl, combine the oats, flour, brown sugar, cinnamon, nutmeg, and salt. Add the butter and use a pastry blender or fork to cut it into pea-size pieces. Refrigerate until ready to use.
3. In a medium bowl, place the fruit and taste, adding the raw cane sugar only if needed to sweeten. Fill each ramekin to the top with fruit, then sprinkle with 3 tablespoons of oat mixture. Bake until the tops are brown and bubbly for 30 to 40 minutes. Set aside to cool for 20 minutes.
4. Top with a dollop of Greek yogurt, drizzle with honey, and serve.

Nutrition Info:

- Info Per Serving: Calories: 294 ;Fat: 10g ;Protein: 5g ;Carbs: 58g .

4-week Diet Plan

Day 1
Breakfast: Omelette With Smoky Shrimp
Lunch: Smoky Scrambled Eggs With Salmon
Dinner: Vegetarian Sloppy Joes

Day 2
Breakfast: No-egg Mushroom Frittata
Lunch: Lamb Shanks Braised Under Pressure
Dinner: Teriyaki Vegetable Stir-fry

Day 3
Breakfast: Morning Naan Bread With Mango Jam
Lunch: Lemon & Caper Turkey Scaloppine
Dinner: Acorn Squash Stuffed With Beans & Spinach

Day 4
Breakfast: Breakfast Bake Millet With Blueberry
Lunch: Magnificent Herbaceous Pork Meatballs
Dinner: Matcha-infused Tofu Rice

Day 5
Breakfast: Ginger Banana Smoothie
Lunch: Chuck Roasted Spicy Beef With Broccoli Curry
Dinner: Oat & Chickpea Patties With Avocado Dip

Day 6
Breakfast: Tropical Smoothie Bowl
Lunch: Korean Vegetable Salad With Smoky Crispy Kalua Pork
Dinner: Cashew & Chickpea Curry

Day 7
Breakfast: Coconut & Raspberry Crêpes
Lunch: Veggie & Beef Brisket
Dinner: Traditional Cilantro Pilaf

Day 8
Breakfast: Fantastic Fruit Cereal
Lunch: Pan-fried Turkey Meatballs
Dinner: Zucchini & Pepper Hash With Fried Eggs

Day 9
Breakfast: Strawberry & Pecan Breakfast
Lunch: Saucy Tomato Beef Meatballs
Dinner: Pesto Mushroom Pizza

Day 10
Breakfast: Sweet Kiwi Oatmeal Bars
Lunch: Paleo Turkey Thighs With Mushroom
Dinner: Full Of Flavour Braised Bok Choy With Shiitake Mushrooms

Day 11
Breakfast: Gluten-free And Dairy-free Little Fruit Muffins
Lunch: Mustardy Beef Steaks
Dinner: American-style Tempeh With Garden Peas

Day 12
Breakfast: Coconut Porridge With Strawberries
Lunch: Gingered Beef Stir-fry With Peppers
Dinner: Amazing Toasted Cumin Crunch

Day 13
Breakfast: Simple Apple Muffins
Lunch: Chicken A La Tuscana
Dinner: Favourite Pizza With Quinoa Flatbread

Day 14
Breakfast: Avocado, Kale & Cauliflower Bowl
Lunch: Tangy Beef Carnitas
Dinner: Feels Like Autumn Loaf With Root Vegetable

Day 15

Breakfast: Maple Crêpes
Lunch: Hot & Spicy Beef Chili
Dinner: Salad-like Green Smoothie

Day 16

Breakfast: Yummy Gingerbread Oatmeal
Lunch: Classic Sunday Pot Roast
Dinner: Tangy Nutty Brussel Sprout Salad

Day 17

Breakfast: Spicy Apple Pancakes
Lunch: Chicken Satay
Dinner: Traditional Lebanese Salad

Day 18

Breakfast: Morning Matcha & Ginger Shake
Lunch: Rosemary Pork Loin
Dinner: Maple Walnut & Pear Salad

Day 19

Breakfast: Home-style Turkey Burgers
Lunch: Filling Casserole With Cabbage And Sausage
Dinner: Low In Calories Salad With Artichoke And Almond

Day 20

Breakfast: Lime Salmon Burgers
Lunch: Golden, Crispy, Buttery Pan-seared Cod
Dinner: Complementary Spinach Salad

Day 21

Breakfast: Sneaky Fiery Veggie Burgers
Lunch: Rich Grandma's Salmon Chowder
Dinner: High-spirited Salmon Salad

Day 22

Breakfast: Hot Lentil Tacos With Guacamole
Lunch: Halibut Al Ajillo
Dinner: Lemony Spinach Salad

Day 23

Breakfast: Tofu Caprese Casserole
Lunch: Asian-inspired Salmon
Dinner: Orange & Kale Salad

Day 24

Breakfast: Black Bean Burgers
Lunch: Good Old-fashioned Mackerel Risotto
Dinner: Refreshingly Spicy Chicken Salad With Cumin And Mango

Day 25

Breakfast: Tofu Loaf With Nuts
Lunch: Scallops With Capers
Dinner: The Best Mediterranean Salad

Day 26

Breakfast: Ultimate Burger With Hummus
Lunch: Honey-mustard Salmon
Dinner: Carrot & Cabbage Salad With Avocado

Day 27

Breakfast: Autenthic Salmon Ceviche
Lunch: Salmon & Asparagus Parcels
Dinner: Warm Collard Salad

Day 28

Breakfast: Lovable Smoothie With Coconut And Ginger
Lunch: Pan-seared Salmon Au Pistou
Dinner: Mushroom & Wild Rice Salad

INDEX

A

B

C

Classic Vegetarian Tagine 79
Coconut & Raspberry Crêpes 14
Coconut Chia Pudding 83
Coconut Porridge With Strawberries 16
Colourful Fiesta Guacamole 63
Commercial And Mild Curry Powder 63
Complementary Spinach Salad 55
Crunchy And Creamy Pistachio Smoothie 48
Curry Soup With Butternut Squash And Coconut 77

D

Dairy Free Apple Cider Vinegar With Tangy Barbecue Sauce 66
Delectable Multivitamin Smoothie 51
Delicious Nutmeg Muffins With Vanilla And Blueberries 80
Delicious Pesto With Kale 68
Delicious Proteinaceous Smoothie 53
Delightful Smoothie With Apple And Honey 53
Diverse Salad With Shredded Root Vegetable 61

E

Easy Garbanzo Soup 74

F

Fancy Cod Stew With Cauliflower 35
Fantastic Fruit Cereal 15
Fantastic Green Salad 60
Favourite Pizza With Quinoa Flatbread 45
Feels Like Autumn Loaf With Root Vegetable 46
Fennel & Parsnip Bisque 71
Filling Casserole With Cabbage And Sausage 28
Flavourful Shrimp And Grits 35
For Beginners Juice With Granny Smith Apples 50
French Peasant Turkey Stew 76
Fresh Berry Smoothie With Ginger 47
Fresh Maple Dressing 65
Fresh Minty Punch With Peach 50
Fruity One For All Smoothie 49
Full Of Flavour Braised Bok Choy With Shiitake Mushrooms 42
Full Of Spice And Zesty Rub 67

G

H

I

K

L

M

Magnificent Herbaceous Pork Meatballs 21

Mango Halibut Curry 33

Maple Crêpes 17

Maple Walnut & Pear Salad 55

Marinated Greek Dressing 70

Matcha-infused Tofu Rice 38

Mediterranean Green On Green Smoothie 51

Mediterranean Salmon 34

Mid Afternoon Grilled Banana And Homemade Nut Butter 86

Minty Juice With Pineapple And Cucumber 52

Minty Salad With Melon 62

Mixed Berry Smoothie With Acai 52

Mixed Mushroom Soup 75

Morning Matcha & Ginger Shake 19

Morning Naan Bread With Mango Jam 13

Moroccan Inspired Lentil Soup 74

Mushroom & Wild Rice Salad 60

Mustardy Beef Steaks 25

Must-have Ranch Dressing 65

N

Natural Crispy Seasonal Fruits 87

Natural Dressing With Ginger And Turmeric 69

Nightshade Free Cinnamon Pecans 85

No-egg Mushroom Frittata 12

Nutritional Sauce With Tofu And Basil 68

O

Oat & Chickpea Patties With Avocado Dip 39

Oatmeal Chocolate Cookies 84

Omelette With Smoky Shrimp 12

Orange & Kale Salad 57

P

Paleo Turkey Thighs With Mushroom 25

Pan-fried Turkey Meatballs 23

Pan-seared Salmon Au Pistou 32

Peppery Soup With Tomato 79

Pesto Mushroom Pizza 42

Pumpkin & Garbanzo Chili With Kale 72

R

Raisin Oatmeal Biscuits 82

Refreshingly Spicy Chicken Salad With Cumin And Mango 58

Rich Grandma's Salmon Chowder 29

Roasted Basil & Tomato Soup 75

Roasted-pumpkin Soup 78

Rosemary Pork Loin 28

S

Salad-like Green Smoothie 47

Salmon & Asparagus Parcels 32

Saucy And Natural Flavoured Golden Seared Scallops With Wilted Bacon Spinach 36

Saucy Tomato Beef Meatballs 24

Scallops With Capers 31

Sea Scallops In Citrus Dressing 33

Seared Trout With Greek Yogurt Sauce 34

Sicilian Papaya Sorbet 82

Simple Apple Muffins 17

Smoky Scrambled Eggs With Salmon 19

Smooth Butternut Squash Smoothie 48

Sneaky Fiery Veggie Burgers 40

Sour Cream With Lemon And Dill 64

Soy-free Salad With Chopped Chicken And Apple 62

Spiced Chai With Baked Apples 81

Spicy Apple Pancakes 18

Spicy Turkey Soup 71

Stomach Soothing Smoothie With Green Apple 51

Strawberry & Pecan Breakfast 15

Super Simple Stew With Mango And Black Bean 72

Sweet Kiwi Oatmeal Bars 15

T

Tangy Beef Carnitas 26

Tangy Nutty Brussel Sprout Salad 54

Teriyaki Vegetable Stir-fry 37

The Best Mediterranean Salad 58

Thyme Pumpkin Stir-fry 18

Timeless Fruit Cocktail And Rose Water Yogurt 80

To Die For Homemade Mayonnaise 67

Tofu Caprese Casserole 41

Tofu Loaf With Nuts 44

Traditional And Delightful Gremolata Sauce 64